Trump Derangement Syndrome
or
Democratic Narcissism:
You Decide

by

Bea Cearnach

Dedication

This book is dedicated to Dan Bongino, whose selfless hard work and amazing podcasts inspired this work and encouraged me to get some "skin in the game. "Kudos Dan! History will thank you for helping preserve our great nation. I would also like to express appreciation to 21st century superheroes: Congressman Devin Nunes and Admiral Michael Rogers. I would also like to say a big thank you to Sara Carter, Sean Hannity, Judge Jeanine and Laura Ingraham for all their hard work and professional journalism. Lastly, I would like to thank President Donald J. Trump. Never has anyone faced such venom for serving the American people. Thank you for your grit and backbone. You are truly inspirational! Finally, thank you to my family for being patient with me while I wrote this book. Let's go get ice-cream!

Contents

Introduction – Narcissus: Ancient History's 1st Selfie Addict

Once upon a time, there was a hunter named Narcissus. Narcissus was known to all because he was incredibly handsome. Son of a god and a nymph, the young, Greek man broke hearts wherever he went. Many tried to win his love, but Narcissus rejected every overture. One lovely nymph, Echo, fell for this well-put-together lad, and followed him throughout the forest. When he discovered her, Narcissus rejected her outright. Devastated, Echo wandered the forest for the rest of her days. All that remained of Echo was the sound of her trailing voice among the trees.

Narcissus' behavior was reported to Nemesis, the Greek god of revenge. She decided to punish Narcissus. She led him to a pool of water in the forest. When Narcissus saw his reflection in the pool, he fell in love with himself immediately. He had finally found someone worthy of his love. He could not bear to look away from his own beautiful reflection. He became history's first official selfie addict. He died at this pool, some claiming that he had committed suicide from despair. He had realized that no one was as worthy as he was for his own love. Others claimed that while trying to kiss his own reflection, Narcissus fell in the pool and drowned. The corpse of Narcissus was found later by the side of the pool. It had been transformed into beautiful flowers: The Narcissus or Daffodils. These flowers forever bear his name and are associated with the coming of spring.

Narcissus taking the first ancient selfie

Chapter 1
Trump Derangement Syndrome or Something Else?

During the election and first year of President Donald Trump in office, many unusual behaviors have been observed from Democratic or liberal citizens of the United States of America. Behaviors ranged from rolling on the ground in rage or disbelief, catatonic retreat to safe spaces, and/or unrealistic denial of election results. The Mainstream News Media, ever devoted to selling stories and advertisement clicks, have fueled these behaviors by repeated coverage. Are these behaviors because of President Trump or is something else going on?

President Trump, pre-election, was not a threatening person. His TV show, The Apprentice, enjoyed favorable ratings on NBC; it was the seventh-most-watched show in its first year in 2004. He had appeared in G-rated children's movies such Home Alone. Apart from his very public divorce in 1992 to his wife, Ivanna, he experienced sporadic media coverage. He built hotels, golf courses and casinos while the rest of the world went about their business.

In 2016, President Trump announced his intention to run for the executive office. Everyone remembers the epic descent on the golden escalator with his gorgeous wife, Melania, in Trump Towers to announce his candidacy. The outsider and non-politician proclaimed his intention to govern America with a practical, business-minded approach.

Few took Donald Trump's presidential run seriously at first. Debates came and went. Republicans, Democrats and Liberals doubted that the campaign would go far. Then, Donald Trump beat the odds. He won the Electoral College in a landslide. Signs of Trump Derangement Syndrome were evident within twenty-four hours. Democratic supporters were seen wailing, rolling, marching and exhibiting extreme outbursts of disappointment at losing.

Everyone knows the disappointment of an election loss if politics is followed long enough. The winds of politics shift, usually every other election. The Democratic response of the election of Donald Trump was, however, different and somewhat troubling. The denial of results, the refusal to give up power, and the ongoing activity to indict the President with illegal activity to remove him from office has been concerning. It reveals a deeper problem. It demonstrates a condition that many such Democrats seem to suffer from: Democratic Narcissism. Conservative news media have named the recent, bizarre Democratic behavior Trump Derangement Syndrome. Inexplicably, Liberals and Democrats have been acting irrationally since that 2016 election. Trump Derangement Syndrome, or TDS, is a sarcastic psychologist diagnosis, to explain the frenzied and hostile behavior of people directed at anything related to President Donald Trump or his presidency.

Why have Liberals and Democrats acted (and are acting) this way? Was it something President Trump said or did?

My theory is that President Trump is not the direct cause of this peculiar Trump Derangement Syndrome behavior. This book is really **not** about him. Democrats enjoyed eight years of unfettered power under the Obama presidency. They became sold on themselves and their policies during their reign. Historically, they had already been praising themselves for protecting the "little guy." In recent decades, they portrayed themselves as "defenders" of the higher moral ground while instigating their own entitlement. The election of President Trump put an end to this rule. The Reign was challenged and defeated by POPULAR VOTE. President Donald Trump was

subsequently perceived to be the roadblock of all
Democratic objectives and self-adulation. Democratic
Liberals, like narcissists, became desperate to return to
their self-proclaiming and self- affirming kingdom, ignoring
the will of the electorate at that time.

What is Narcissism? Narcissism is a personality disorder.
It is characterized by self-love. The average Narcissist is
not an easy person to live with. He (or she) perpetually
talks about himself, boasting long lists of achievements.
Most times, these achievements are exaggerated. The
Narcissist feels superior to others and boasts of power,
brilliance insight that only few can share or keep up with.
They thrive on and demand constant praise. A Narcissist
is entitled. Because they are superior to the surrounding
population, they feel as though they deserve only the very
best: cars, houses, vacations, supermodel mates and
special favors. A Narcissist can be very expensive to live
with.

The average narcissist has difficulty in maintaining
long-term relationships. Because they are busy talking and
thinking about themselves, they lack empathy and
understanding of others. They are incredibly demanding,
often belittling their significant others by criticizing their
flaws. The narcissist will sometimes manipulate of others

by gaslighting them. (More on that in Chapters 7 & 8) They are envious of people who have things that they don't, especially if they feel entitled to the object in question. For a myriad of causes, narcissistic relationships suffer or are extinguished all together.

Rage is a common indicator of a narcissist. It occurs when dreams are not realized or a contender dares to challenge the narcissist reign of power. A narcissist is highly sensitive to criticism and behaves much like an outraged toddler not getting his or her way. Special favors must be granted without question. If for any reason the narcissist is not placated, Hiroshima results.

The narcissist is an extremely insecure person. When the fog and mirrors have cleared, a fragile person, racked with self-doubt and feelings of inner emptiness, emerges. This person, so intent on exposing the flaws of others, lives in fear of being the reject himself. He creates a smokescreen of distraction so that no one can discover hidden shortcomings. Much like magician behind the curtain in The Wizard of Oz, the narcissist will jump through many hoops to prevent the average bystander from making the discovery of the true fragile identity behind the mask.

Is a person born with Narcissism Personality Disorder? The cause of this disorder is not known but is generally considered to be learned behavior. Some clinicians believe that the disorder develops when parents significantly misunderstand their child during childhood years. These parents criticized or degraded their children until they could no longer tolerate any self-criticism.

With counseling, the narcissist can learn new behaviors and replace negative core beliefs with more positive ones. I have personal experience with Narcissism Personality Disorder. I was raised by a narcissistic father. Although I am not a health care professional, I can detect a narcissist almost immediately. This awareness has been sharpened because of years of personal suffering. Once one is familiar with what baseline narcissistic behavior looks like, it is easy to spot a narcissist in different settings and circumstances. I propose that such behavior has been exhibited by Democratic Liberals since the Presidential election of Donald Trump in 2016.

It is not a light thing to suggest that anyone is a narcissist. The continued behaviors of Democrats and liberals at the election of President Trump, however, have been disturbing. Many parallels exist between the actions of Democrats and those actions of people who suffer from

Narcissism Personality Disorder. These reactions are significant and deeply worrisome. The election of Donald Trump merely revealed a wide spectrum of narcissistic behavior that was pre-existent. After reading the following pages, you decide. Is recent behavior isolated to Trump Derangement Syndrome and the results of a one-time, presidential election or is it a deeper, systemic and societal problem?

Chapter 2
And the Award Goes To…

Hollywood actors have been viciously critical of President Donald J. Trump since his election in 2017. Meryl Streep, Jimmy Kimmel, Alec Baldwin, Chelsea Handler, Chrissy Teigen and John Legend and a cast of hundreds have also jumped onto the Trump-Bashing Bandwagon for the world to hear and see. What seems to threaten them?

Celebrities accuse Mr. Trump of promoting violence, abusing the American people, and endangering citizen's lives across America. What causes these unsubstantiated beliefs? Has Trump murdered people while in office? Has he sent out FBI agents against US citizens, Gestapo-style? Labeled by these actors as a dangerous racist, President Trump has not enacted any laws targeting race. African Americans and Hispanics have only benefited from record low unemployment levels because of his economic policies. Why are these celebrities acting this way? Why are they suffering from Trump Derangement Syndrome?

Could the root of this Hollywood dysfunction be rooted in a deeply-rooted and pre-existent disorder of Narcissism? Narcissists demand a steady stream of praise and attention. Hollywood actors perform for ratings and notice. They demand accolades for their "hard work" of acting accomplishments. They often feel that they are a superior people group, called to lead their ignorant audiences to a 'higher" consciousness and vision. Appreciation must accompany this mission. Hollywood actors roll like a self-proclaimed, super race-- especially while proclaiming an often times liberal agenda. The result is praise, praise and even more praise. If actors are not straight-out narcissists themselves, they certainly live and breathe in a culture of self-lauding narcissism.

George Clooney gave an interesting acceptance speech when he won Best Supporting Actor in 2006 for his film, Syriana. In his acceptance, Clooney boasted that Hollywood was out of touch with reality and he was proud of this fact. He congratulated himself to be part of this group who the world needed to speak out and lead them into just causes. He stated:

And finally, I would say that, you know, we are a little bit out of touch in Hollywood every once in a while, I think. It's probably a good thing. We're the ones who talked about AIDS when it was just being whispered, and we talked about civil rights when it wasn't really popular. And we, you know, we bring up subjects, we are the ones—this

Academy, this group of people gave Hattie McDaniel an Oscar in 1939 when blacks were still sitting in the backs of theaters. I'm proud to be a part of this Academy, proud to be part of this community, and proud to be out of touch. And I thank you so much for this.

While the cause of African American Civil Liberty is noble, who chose George Clooney along with fellow thespians as the spokespeople of modern day society? George Clooney never suffered because of the denial of his civil rights as real-life heroes like Martin Luther King, Rosa Parks and other brave African Americans did. Clooney's message is not wrong. He was again doing what came naturally: acting in a role. It is interesting, however, how actors in Hollywood have elevated themselves as critics of the society that they are merely imitating.

Hollywood abounds with actors who espouse the beliefs of the Democrat Party or of Liberalism. These entertainers also love to give each other awards. The Hollywood success is based on being watched, it is not surprising that narcissists could be spawned from such an environment. The Oscars, the Grammys, the People's Choice, the Baftas, MTV's, the VMAs, and the Billboards are some of the award opportunities where glittering stars praise each other in this mutual appreciation society. Each film year, hundreds of awards are given out to the most beautiful and the best- further reinforcing the spectrum of narcissistic dysfunction present.

The acceptance speeches heard during these awards ceremonies are many times self-centered. At the inception of the Academy Awards, the actor or actress was expected to demurely accept the Oscar in humility. They were expected to express deep gratitude to the Academy and not draw excessive attention to themselves beyond lavish clothing choices. The Hollywood elitist bubble has since changed that expectation significantly. Pathological, self-satisfaction increases during these ceremonies from year to year.

If rivers do not flow from star tear ducts on Academy Award night, self-applauding affirmations do. (Acceptance speech guidelines recommend a forty-five second duration.) Sally Field's acceptance speech in 1984 is a case in point. Ms. Fields won the Best Actress Award in the 1984 movie, Places of the Heart. Her second Oscar, in this film, she played a 1930's widow in the South who struggled to save farm from foreclosure. Sally did not struggle, however, with congratulating herself hysterically during her acceptance speech. First, she thanked her family for having patience with her, *"for this obsession of*

ME." She then continued to exclaim to the audience, *"you like me, you really, really like me, you like me, right now, you like me!"* Sally seemed to be validating her self-worth based on this "coveted" award.

As the stars parade on red carpets of honor, their award acceptance speeches often morph into liberal platforms of social justice. Actor-activists heap further praise to themselves because they "care" about political opinions. Issues that the stars highlight include gender inequality, sexual harassment in the #MeToo movement, gun violence, and DACA. The more left-leaning the cause, the greater the praise.

While there is no official tally of Hollywood Democrats or Liberals, there are approximately 240,000 entertainment related jobs according to a recent Otis Report on the Creative Economy of the Los Angeles region. Of that number, conservatives in the industry are estimated to be as high as a few thousand. (Los Angeles Times, In Liberal Hollywood, A Conservative Minority Faces a Backlash in the Age of Trump, David Ng, March 11, 2017) If 3000 actors, for example, are tallied hypothetically, that puts Conservative entertainers in the 1.25% percentile and Democrat/Liberal entertainers in the 98.75% majority of the Hollywood population. Such celebrities could create

Celebrity Fitness Body Pump Workout with their weighty award hardware. Narcissist Spectrum issues remain intact.

Notable Celebrity Narcissism Quotes:

<u>James Cameron</u>
"I'm the king of the world!" James Cameron, when he received the Oscar for Best Director for Titanic, 1998. It is understandable that Cameron is happy that he won, but really?

<u>Jared Leto</u>
"To all the dreamers out there in the world watching this tonight, in places like the Ukraine and Venezuela, I want to say that we are here. And as you struggle to make your dreams happen; to live the impossible, we're thinking of you tonight." Jared Leto, Best Supporting Actor, Dallas Buyers Club, 2013.

It is wonderful to acknowledge the sufferings of the citizens of the Ukraine and Venezuela to promote awareness, but to assume that the downtrodden are watching the Award ceremony while experiencing severe oppression is bizarre. Do they even have televisions, let alone the freedom to watch TV without government control of the airwaves? This statement is proof positive of an elitist Hollywood bubble.

Leto went on that evening to congratulate himself on his activism. He reported after the ceremony that as an award winner, *"you have an opportunity when you stand on this stage. You can make it about yourself or you can hold up a mirror and shine a light and that's what I chose to do tonight. I mean, because of Thirty Seconds to Mars, because I'm in a band, how many people are here from outside of the -- of the USA? Quite a few of you. Okay. Good. I'm at home then. But I feel at home all over the world. And you know, for me, these global issues impact us in a really direct way."* (Wow. Just wow.)

Madonna

"I am my own experiment. I am my own work of art...I'm tough, ambitious and I know exactly what I want. If that makes me a b_tch, okay" Enough said, right there. Madonna has been particularly vicious towards President Donald Trump in her expressed hatred of him.

Kanye West

"I am the nucleus...the greatest pain in life is that I will never be able to see myself perform live." Everyone loves

Kanye. At least this celebrity thinks for himself and wore a MAGA hat to stir up his fellow entertainers.

Kim Kardashian West
"I love a selfie in the mirror… stretch marks are like my biggest fear in life!" The Undisputed Selfie Queen, Kim uploads daily photos of herself and her life to social media. Kim is truly beautiful. What is harmful is a narcissist who imitates such behavior to gain self-validation via likes on Instagram. This world is not real, but virtual. Kim just launched a perfume bottle in the shape of her own naked body. Kim clearly wants her assets to be noticed. Who does that?

Karl Lagerfeld
"Vanity is the healthiest thing in life." (Really?)

David Lee Roth
"I'm not conceited. Conceit is a fault and I have no faults." He must be the best David Roth in the whole world or the only David Roth in the whole world.

Lady Gaga
"I live for applause… I'm already crazy. I'm a fearless person. I think it creeps up on you. I don't think it can be stopped. If my destiny is to lose my mind because of fame,

then that's my destiny. But my passion still means more than anything." Lady Gaga, at least, is an artist and not an imitation of one. Lady Gaga's shocking outfits are also designed to attract symbolic attention and make a statement.

<u>Miley Cyrus</u>
"I take selfies to know that I am alive…it's time for this queen to find another throne." Miley has demonstrated some very odd behavior and pole-dancer-like dance moves while finding herself. This poor girl seems desperate to prove that she is no longer a Disney poster child.

One does not have to wait long to hear a celebrity A-lister express a narcissistic-sounding statement. Divas, rock stars, and other performers also enjoy being regularly honored and applauded. Entire books could be filled with outrageous Hollywood quotes of self-love and self-importance. Narcissism compounds, however, when the such a person takes up a cause. The result of any praise culture can end very badly- many times in rehab. Despite the negative consequences, the Hollywood/ celebrity narcissists "soldier on" with the good news of what they are doing for mankind. Many people wish they would stick to acting and entertaining, so they would not have to pretend to take them seriously.

Imagine for a moment what would happen if a Hollywood celebrity was not praised or applauded on a regular basis. Worse, how long would he or she make it on an Awards Fast? (What would that sort of cleanse look like?) My guess is that there would not be enough psychologist couches to accommodate them all. It is also interesting to see how Democratic/Liberal politicians gel so well with Hollywood narcissists. They share much common limelight while highlighting social issues. Together, they discover their respective niches on the Narcissistic Spectrum- a shared journey, so to speak. Ask such celebrities of what they think of Conservative actors or political causes and they readilare sure to give listeners an earful.

Madonna is one of the most antagonistic stars to speak out against the President, Trump Derangement-style. At the Women's March in January 2017, she threatened, *"Yes, I have thought an awful lot about blowing up the White House…It took this horrific moment of darkness to wake us the f-kup."* Madonna ended her speech that day with a parody of her song, "Express Yourself," in which she sang, *"Donald Trump, suck a d--k, I'm not your b---h."* Cher, another outspoken celebrity, shared Madonna's animosity for President Trump when she said, *"He doesn't mean we want to 'Make America Great Again.' He means: We want to make America straight and white… I'm here for multiple reasons, one out of fear because I'm so frightened for what's going to happen to this particular (LGBT) community. I know there's going to be other people, other minorities that are going to be totally screwed as well, but I honestly fear for your safety."*

Why do these two women react this way? Why do they fear Donald Trump? They state that they do not feel safe with him and hate him to the point of violence. Cher, however, during a Mardi Gras interview in Sydney, Australia admitted that she had never really met him and stated, *"I was at a party where he was once, but I don't think I would have gone out of my way to meet him. And he probably wouldn't either, I'm not his type of girl."* (Cher on why Trump Blocked Her on Twitter, Hating her Age, Playing Mardi Gras and Her Fave Emoticon, Cameron Adams, News.Com.Au, March 1, 2018).

Madonna met President Trump once and seemed, by her own words, to like him: *"I wouldn't call him a friend or anything, but I've certainly met him. I did a photo shoot years ago at [Trump's] Mar-a-Lago in Palm Beach [Fla.] for a Versace campaign. He's a very friendly guy,*

-charismatic in that boastful, macho, alpha-male way. I found his political incorrectness amusing. Of course, I didn't know he was going to be running for president 20 years later. People like that exist in the world, I'm OK with it." (Billboard 'Woman of the Year' Madonna Gives Provocative Interview on Everything From 2016 Election to Ageism, Billboard, Elizabeth Banks, December 5, 2016).

If neither of these women had met President Trump nor spent serious time getting to know him, why did they become violent in Trump Derangement Syndrome, call him names and threaten to blow him up in the White House?

Democratic Narcissism could be the root of the strong feelings of celebrity women. Madonna and Cher are also Hollywood champions of Democratic/Liberal causes. They seek to lead society into understanding and awareness and, life fellow Hollywood A-listers, expect appreciation for these efforts. They are accustomed to huge followings and devoted fan bases that elevate them to goddess status.

There is only one problem in this scenario. Donald Trump does not worship people or celebrities. He doesn't need them. He is not moved by posturing or threats. He is not anti-gay, anti-women, or anti-much of anything. Donald

Trump is, however, a self-made man who values people for their individual accomplishments over their words. Because he is a billionaire, he cannot be bought. Donald Trump would, therefore, not be likely to sing praises for these women's praises or swoon before them as their average fans would. This alone could send any average narcissist into blind rage.

Celebrity hatred of President Trump is illogical. Up until he announced his candidacy, President Trump was a himself a celebrity- accepted, at least for his money, in their circles. Celebrities and Donald Trump frequented each other's parties and weddings. There are numerous photos of President Trump with many of his most vocal Hollywood critics. They did not criticize Trump's liquor when they drank it freely or his hospitality when it was offered to them. Pull the praise from a narcissist and watch unpleasant substances hit the fan.

Chapter 3
A Narcissist and Failure

One hallmark characteristic of a person suffering from Narcissist Personality Disorder is the inability to admit failure. The narcissist is always right, and faults are neither possible or acceptable. Democratic Liberals seem to share this problem. One need only look to the example of Hillary Clinton on Election Night of 2017 to observe this tendency.

Polls and pundits predicted that Hillary Clinton would win the 2017 Presidential Election in a landslide. The Mainstream Media concurred. Donald Trump didn't seem to have a hope. The problem was, contrary to polling data, that Trump won the Electoral College in landslide victory. When the results were announced, Hillary Clinton went missing in action. Hours passed before Hillary gave her concession speech. Outgoing President Obama was forced to telephone Hillary to urge her to make the concession speech. Hillary had failed to break her Glass Ceiling. Granted, the election results must have been inconceivable for her to accept, but what followed afterwards was clearly deranged behavior brought on by the election of Donald Trump. (TDS)

After lying low for a few weeks, Hillary Clinton began to publicly reflect on the causes of her election defeat. She primarily blamed others of causing her election defeat. The list of people she has blamed for her loss is long:

- The FBI
- James Comey, Former Head of the FBI
- Vladimir Putin
- Anti-American forces
- Anyone who assumed that she would win
- Low information voters
- Bad polling numbers
- Obama winning two terms
- People wanting change
- Misogynists
- Suburban women
- The New York Times
- Television Executives
- Cable News
- Netflix
- Democrats not making the right documentaries
- Facebook
- Twitter
- Wikileaks
- Fake news
- Content farms in Macedonia

· The Republican Party
· The Democrat Party

This list continues to grow with each Hillary Clinton book signing or public speaking engagement. In her book, <u>What Happened</u>, Hillary Clinton asks, "What makes me such a lightning rod for fury? I'm really asking. I'm at a loss," she writes. "I think it's partly because I'm a woman." Here, Mrs. Clinton wrestles to make sense of how she lost the 2017 Presidential Election. Why did voters not choose her? Why were they often mad at her? Mystified, she identifies the real reason for her loss: she was a woman.

Mrs. Clinton in this quote is clearly in denial. Many in America have looked forward to the day when a woman would be elected as the President of the United States. Credentials, campaign platforms and service records, however, are also critically important to voters. It seems incredible that Mrs. Clinton did not factor that reality into the above quote.

Narcissists generally avoid responsibility for their actions. They enjoy worthy causes, especially if they are receiving much attention or praise for participating in them. They don't like it, however, when others impose responsibility on them. Narcissists interpret such impositions as attempts to control their freedom. How do they escape accountability?

According to Licensed Mental Health Counselor, Christine Hammond (Psyche Central, May 7, 2017), narcissists use seven tactics to escape responsibility:

1. Intimidate/Blame
The narcissist begins by bullying a person, trying to make them accountable to him. Frequently, he will call their subject names and belittle to assert his dominance. Once a subordinate position has been established, the narcissist will blame his for attempting to make him look bad.

2. Accuse/Project
To circumvent any accountability, the narcissist preempts attack by accusing another person. Usually they pick a codependent-type person who is likely to idolize the narcissist. Then, the narcissist projects problems he is answerable for onto the that person. He then cuts out after making his projection.

3. Argue/Exhaust
This tactic gives immediate results. When confronted, the narcissist picks one small detail and argues it to the

minute degree. If the other person argues back, they pick another tiny point to endlessly wear down their opponent. Exhausted, frustrated, and annoyed, the victim gives up making the narcissist responsible for what he does.

4. Deny/Rewrite
After denying responsibility, the narcissist will try to rewrite history. He will say that he was forced into being held responsible when they volunteered in the first place. This tactic often leaves the victim questioning themselves and their memory.

5. Fear/Avoid
A Narcissist will take a person's fear and turn it into paranoia. He turns on his charm to cause harm by creating a believable story with scary outcome. Once the subject is frightened, the narcissist will accuse that the other person is reactionary and any anything the other person asks for should be ignored.

In conclusion, the narcissist is unable to accept responsibility for his or her own failures or shortcomings. They devise smokescreens and mirrors to detract from their failures. Facing defeat forces him or her to accept that they have fallen short. This realization is unacceptable.

Traits of narcissism are identifiable in the following quotes from What Happened, Hillary Clinton's personal memoirs on why specifically she lost the 2017 Presidential election:

Mrs. Clinton blamed her election loss on Bernie Sanders:

"Nonetheless, his attacks caused lasting damage, making it harder to unify progressives in the general election and paving the way for Trump's 'Crooked Hillary' campaign. I don't know if that bothered Bernie or not. He certainly shared my horror at the thought of Donald Trump becoming President, and I appreciated that he campaigned for me in the general election. But he isn't a Democrat—that's not a smear, that's what he says. He didn't get into the race to make sure a Democrat won the White House, he got in to disrupt the Democratic Party." Bernie Sanders wanted to be the President because he wanted to disrupt Democrats or because he wanted to be the President? It is unlikely that he ran to be a destructive force to the political party that he had been committed to for decades. Mrs. Clinton blamed her election loss on Vladimir Putin: "What would I have done? There's nothing I was looking forward to more than showing Putin that his efforts to influence our election and

install a friendly puppet had failed. Our first face-to-face meeting would really have been something. I know he must be enjoying everything that's happened instead."

Mrs. Clinton alleged in this quote that it was Vladimir Putin who was responsible for her election defeat. Putin had "installed" President Trump in her place. She continues to maintain this narrative despite the numerous investigations that concluded no such collusion between President Trump and Vladimir Putin ever occurred.

Mrs. Clinton blamed her election loss on Jill Stein of the Green Party:

"A small but still significant number of left-wing voters may well have thrown the election to Trump. Jill Stein, the Green Party candidate, called me and my policies 'much scarier than Donald Trump' and praised his pro-Russia stance. This isn't surprising, considering that Stein sat with Putin and Michael Flynn at the infamous Moscow dinner in 2015 celebrating the Kremlin's propaganda network RT, and later said she and Putin agreed 'on many issues'… "in each state, there were more than enough Stein voters to swing the result, just like Ralph Nader did in Florida and New Hampshire in 2000. Maybe, like actress Susan

Sarandon, Stein thinks electing Trump will hasten 'the revolution.' Who knows?"

It is rare for any Democrat to throw any environmentally friendly, Green Party leader under the bus. However, Mrs. Clinton did just that when she accused Ms. Stein of colluding with Mr. Trump and Putin to cost her the election.

Mrs. Clinton blamed the Matt Lauer of the NBC Today Show for her election defeat:

"Trump should have reported [Lauer's] performance as an in-kind contribution. Later, there were rumors ginned up by fake news reports that I was so mad at him I stormed off stage, threw a tantrum, and shattered a water glass. While I didn't do any of that, I can't say I didn't fantasize about shaking some sense into Lauer while I was out there... Later, I watched Lauer soft-pedal Trump's interview."

Matt Lauer, in this interview, brought up specific concerns that Bernie Sanders had about Mrs. Clinton's ability to lead as President of the United States. Bernie Sanders criticized that Mrs. Clinton was not qualified to be President because she had received 15 million dollars from Wall Street, voted for the disastrous war in Iraq, and

that she supported trade agreements that cost Americans millions of jobs. These were legitimate criticisms based on Hillary Clinton's service record while in public office. Mrs. Clinton was clearly angered when Lauer later brought up the mysterious disappearance of her personal emails, along with the possibility of handcuffs and prison.
The interview concluded amicably. Quite frankly, Mr. Lauer was only doing his job. Despite this, Hillary Clinton blamed the loss of the election on this interview, Mr. Lauer. She did NOT blame her record of past activities while in office. If you can't stand the heat…

In fairness to Hillary Clinton, she has accepted some blame in her election loss of 2017. She did confess, "*You can blame the data, blame the message, blame anything you want - but I was the candidate. It was my campaign. Those were my decisions.*" It is difficult to imagine what it is like to lose a Presidential election. Feelings of rejection must be poignant and terrible. Mrs. Clinton, however, does persist in her terrible habit of blaming others on a regular basis for her election loss. In a Democratic narcissistic environment, where failure is inconceivable, shifting blame and avoiding responsibility becomes commonplace.

Hillary Rodham Clinton, <u>What Happened</u>, Simon and Schuster, Inc, NY, 2017

Christine Hammond, MS, MHC, 7 Tactics Narcissists Use to Escape Responsibility, Psyche Central Social Network, May 7, 2016

Chapter 4
Entitlement

Characteristic of Narcissism Personality Disorder is the subject's sense of entitlement. The Narcissist demands special favors and requires that his or her requests are fulfilled without questions. This person is above the law and the standards that normal humans are required to live by. When these demands go unfulfilled or challenged, the result is like an angry toddler throwing himself down in a tantrum in the middle of a grocery store aisle.

President Barack Obama, while in office from 2009-2017 issued 276 executive orders. An executive order is a rule, issued by a president, that has the same enforcement power as a law. President Obama was not the only president to issue such orders; Bill Clinton issued 364 and George Bush issued 291. Executive orders are meant to ease operations in the executive branches and determine executive policy. They are increasingly becoming more and more of a controlling aspect of the Executive Branch, but historically they are not unusual.

The powers of the President are clearly stated in the United States Constitution in Article 2. Because it is seen it so rarely these days, here is the portion of this foundational document that outlines the expressed powers of the President:

The President shall be Commander in Chief of the Army and Navy of the United States, and of the Militia of the several States, when called into the actual Service of the United States; he may require the Opinion, in writing, of the principal Officer in each of the executive Departments, upon any Subject relating to the Duties of their respective Offices, and he shall have Power to Grant Reprieves and Pardons for Offences against the United States, except in Cases of Impeachment.

He shall have Power, by and with the Advice and Consent of the Senate, to make Treaties, provided two thirds of the Senators present concur; and he shall nominate, and by and with the Advice and Consent of the Senate, shall appoint Ambassadors, other public Ministers and Consuls, Judges of the supreme Court, and all other Officers of the United States, whose Appointments are not herein otherwise provided for, and which shall be established by Law: but the Congress may by Law vest the Appointment of such inferior Officers, as they think proper, in the President alone, in the Courts of Law, or in the Heads of Departments. He shall from time to time give to the

Congress Information on the State of the Union, and recommend to their Consideration such Measures as he shall judge necessary and expedient; he may, on extraordinary Occasions, convene both Houses, or either of them, and in Case of Disagreement between them, with Respect to the Time of Adjournment, he may adjourn them to such Time as he shall think proper; he shall receive Ambassadors and other public Ministers; he shall take Care that the Laws be faithfully executed, and shall Commission all the Officers of the United States.

Article 2 of the United States Constitution gives the President power to enforce laws. Government agencies- such as the FBI, Department of Justice, CIA or FDA-are subject to his leadership. He is their ultimate boss. In summary, his powers are limited to the following:

• He is to veto, or reject, a proposal for a law

• He is to appoint federal posts, such as members of government agencies

• He is to negotiate foreign treaties with other countries

• He is to appoint federal judges

• He can grant pardons, or forgiveness, for a crime
The president is not allowed to overstep the above duties. Simply put, he is not permitted to do what the Legislative and Judicial branches of the US government are supposed to do. Oversight of the other two branches of government are doing is known as "Checks and Balances."

Additionally, the President of the United States has permission to issue executive orders. This permission is given by the Congress, which, in turn, has the power to override any executive order issued by the president. Executive orders can be controversial because they are not authorized in the Constitution. The President has bit of wiggle room here, so to speak. Every president since George Washington has issued executive orders. So, what is the big deal about them? How do executive orders work?

George Washington proclaimed the Thanksgiving Holiday by executive order in 1789. Dwight Eisenhower used an executive order to enforce desegregation of public schools in Little Rock, Arkansas in 1957. Abraham Lincoln issued his executive order to enact the Emancipation Proclamation which was justified by means of his wartime powers.

Not all executive orders have ended well, however. Franklin Roosevelt, for example, established Japanese Internment Camps by his executive order during World War II in the USA. Harry Truman used an executive order to force private steel mills to remain open during the Korean War. The Supreme Court determined Truman's executive order was invalid and overturned it in Youngstown Street and Tube Co. v. Sawyer in 1952.

President Obama, like his predecessors, also issued many executive orders. These were executive orders with a difference, however. Obama seemed to link his orders with his own personal legacy. Often, these orders violated (or was in opposition with) the consent of the Congress. Obama seemed to feel that he was entitled to bypass the Congress if his policies were not implemented quickly enough. He did this by means of a pen and his cell phone. He justified his actions because of "poll numbers." When he lost control of the Senate in 2014, Obama announced: *"We're not just going to be waiting for legislation in order to make sure that we're providing Americans the kind of help they need. I've got a pen and I've got a phone."*

Bypassing Congress? Really? The majority of Obama's executive orders were later reversed because legislators and judges objected to Obama's overreach. Here are just some of Pen and Cellphone Executive Orders that President Obama issued during his presidency:

2008-Obama promised to close Guantanamo Bay Detention Center of international criminals within a year

2009-Obama directed that the US Government could send tax dollars overseas to fund foreign abortions. (Done with a memo in this instance.)

2010-Executive Order 13535-Abortion was federally funded under the Affordable Health Care Mandate

2011-Title IX Obama guidelines enacted which denied due process for accused offenders of sexual assault

2013 -Affordable Healthcare Birth Control Mandate required nuns to give out contraceptives in Catholic healthcare facilities that were federally funded.

2013- Obama directed federal agencies to prepare for climate change.

2014-Obama required public schools to comply with expanded policies of the School Lunch and School

Breakfast including the marketing of food and beverages (outlawing sugar and soda- Michelle Obama's FLOTUS initiative.)

2014 -Obama decided to grant amnesty to 4 million illegal aliens. (This order was blocked by an appeals court.)

2015 -Obama enacts the 40% mandated reduction of greenhouse gases produced by the Federal Government

2015- Clean Water Rule- allowing the EPA control over any farm ditch, puddle or water they decide. (Impacting where construction of buildings, road, oil pipelines, etc. could be built.)

2015 -The halt of coal mining on federal and tribal lands.

2015- Obama introduces his rule setting standards on hydraulic fracturing that led to a reduction of US oil production to help preserve the environment.

2016- Obama allowed the Peace Corps to change its logo.

2016- Obama regulates the EPA to limit methane emissions from the oil and gas industry. 2016- Obama identified climate change as a national security issue.

2017 -Obama ordered that transgender students could use the bathroom of their choice in public schools.

Throughout his presidency, Obama issued an additional twenty-three executive orders on gun control and gun violence in the USA.

Why has President Trump been able to reverse all these executive orders so quickly? This is because when executive orders bypass the US Congress, the actions are easily reversed. Fast is not always the best! Had President Obama approved these actions with the necessary consent of Congress, they would have remained more permanently as law.

Many foreign treaties were also made in the same way by President Obama; they were not ratified by the United States Congress. The Trans Pacific Partnership, the Iran Nuclear Weapons Deal, the International Arms Treaty and the Paris Accord Agreement are just a few. Each of these foreign treaties were similarly broken with ease with the stroke of President Trump's pen.

In summary, President Obama issued executive orders, to control American citizens from their healthcare choices, to gun control, to puddles in their backyard and to what went into school children's lunchboxes. Why did he believe he had a right to such unprecedented overreach? These imperialistic orders were linked with preserving his legacy which included Obamacare, environmental protection, and sexual equality. Despite Constitutional mandates that he was required to obey, President Obama believed that he was entitled to disregard them, especially when they were not legally approved on his timetable. The Washington Post concurred that *the Obama administration did things (through executive action) it had previously determined it could not do legally.*

It has been troubling to read Twitter responses and hear of statements from like-minded Democrats as President Donald Trump systematically reversed Barack Obama's executive orders. As a candidate, Trump promised to *"cancel every unconstitutional executive action, memorandum and order issued by President Obama."* He has been true to his word. Former President Obama has been strangely quiet from his residence in Kalorama, (neighborhood in Washington, DC) on this. Numerous Democrats, however, have become deranged. Nancy Pelosi, former Democratic Speaker of the House of Representatives exclaimed when describing President Trump's tax bill, *"This is Armageddon. This is the end of the world."* Congresswoman Maxine Waters had been equally vocal at the destruction of the Obama dominion saying:

"[African-Americans] fight against this president, and we point out how dangerous he is for this society and for this country, we're fighting for the democracy. We're saying to those who say they're patriotic, but they've turned a blind eye to the destruction that he's about to cause this country."

While President Obama issued his executive orders, it is significant to remember that he had a loyal, political fan base that **enabled** him to carry them out.

In conclusion, a fundamental characteristic of Narcissism Personality Disorder is the subject's sense of entitlement. The narcissist demands special favors and demands his or her requests to be fulfilled without question. A narcissist is not good at waiting for what he or she wants. This person is above the law and certainly above the standards that normal humans are required to abide by. There is something seriously wrong with the belief that a political leader is above the law in such manner. It is called tyranny. Tyranny originates from the belief that a political leader is above the rules. Requests and orders are to be fulfilled just because he or she is entitled.

The posturing of Trump Derangement Syndrome in
Liberal-minded legislators has its precedent.

____

https://lp.hillsdale.edu/free-pocket-constitution/ Editorial,
Trump's Executive Orders Are Nothing Compared to
Obama's 'Pen and Phone' Abuses, Investor's Business
Daily, 2/01/2017

(https://www.investors.com/politics/editorials/dont-like-trum
ps-executive-orders-blame-obamas-pen-and-phone/)

Chapter 5
Rage

Derangement Zones have recently been observed on American university campuses since the election of President Donald J. Trump. Student behavior has been violent. Professors and students have been injured with broken bones and/or lacerations. Fire has been set to power generators and trees. Glass windows have been shattered. Police in riot gear have been sent in to break up unruly student mobs. What would bring about such rage and anger from American college student-our future?

Rage and narcissism often coexist together according to psychoanalyst Sigmund Freud. When a narcissist suspects that his self-worth or self-esteem is threatened, rage is the result. Sigmund Freud described narcissist dynamics in his book, On Narcissism: An Introduction. He described in this book how narcissistic rage erupts from narcissistic injury (or perceived injury) when the importance of what a narcissist believes is brought into question. Self-preservation is *endangered.* Perhaps a motivation has become suspect or worse, revealed. From Civilizations and Its Discontents, Freud states:

"we are threatened with suffering from three directions: from our body, which is doomed to decay..., from the external world which may rage against us with overwhelming and merciless force of destruction, and finally from our relations with other men... This last source is perhaps more painful to use than any other. (p. 77)"

Lastly, according to Freud, narcissistic-related rage exists on a continuum, ranging from **mild irritation** to **violent acts of attack or murder**. This rage often exists in two layers: constant anger towards someone else or self-directed wrath. The destruction of the offenders is imminent.

What has brought on these displays of rage on college campuses? Is it narcissism, Trump Derangement Syndrome or learned behavior? On one hand, most of these recent campus riots occurred after the 2016 election. On the other hand, according to the student petition at Elon University (in 2016), the cause of their riots was not associated directly with the President Trump, but a different source: the *"spreading of dangerous rhetoric."*

Student protests most often occur when Conservative speakers have been invited to speak on college campuses to encourage a diverse thinking. On the night of the scheduled Conservative speech, the one-time occasion degenerates into a flashpoint of conflict. What is the average college protest riot look like?

Trouble begins when a well-known, Conservative speaker is invited to address college students by a campus group of Republicans or Conservatives. Ben Shapiro, Kathleen Parker and Milo Yiannopoulos are examples of Conservative speakers who have been invited to college campuses by special student organizations. Word travels though campus via flyers or word of mouth. Before the speakers have arrived on campus, however, the drama has already begun.

At Kathleen Parker's event, for example, the students petitioned the Elon College administration prior to the date of her speech. Students begged the administration not to allow Ms. Parker to address them because of her *"dangerous rhetoric."* What was this dangerous rhetoric? Student's concerns centered around the topic of Parker's 2008 book: <u>Save the Males: Why Men Matter, Why Women Should Care</u>. This book centered on how feminism has made enemies out of men. Despite the pre-event protest, Ms. Parker spoke and did not experience student backlash. She stated concerning the criticism, *"We don't need free speech for nice things. We don't need it to write Hallmark greeting card messages. ... We need it because we have to be able to hear the worst things. We have to allow people to protest. I appreciate that some students wanted to protest. That is free speech in action."*

At the very least, costly security measures are required to prepare campus police for such events. Costs of Conservative events range between $600,000 to $4 million dollars. Clearly, such expensive security charges would render many conservative campus events unsustainable before they were even scheduled on to the academic calendar.

The Conservative speakers that, however, did make it on to the school event calendar encountered hecklers and assault at the podium. They also witnessed the vandalism of university property. The controversial Milo Yiannopoulos, for example, was invited by a student group of Republicans to speak during Free Speech Week at the University of California, Berkeley in February 2017. Mr. Yiannopoulos was unable to speak because his event was cancelled before it began. Fires had been set. Windows had been smashed. Police fired flash bangs and pepper spray into the rioting crowd.

At a similar protests, bystanders and professors have been injured. Students protest because they claim that the invited speakers are either racist, sexist, promote hate speech or are homophobic. (Mr. Yiannopoulos, an accomplished "provocateur, " could hardly be labeled as anti-gay, however. He is openly a homosexual and an advocate for gay rights.) In the end, the speeches at California Berkeley during Free Speech Week were cancelled because of "logistical issues and safety concerns." Ben Shapiro's speech at California State University was cancelled in similar fashion in February 2016. A speech by Charles Murray, at Middlebury College in March of 2017, was shut down by hundreds of student hecklers during his speech. Later the students pushed and shoved Mr. Murray in the hallway as he tried to leave the building. Other speakers cancelled for private or graduation speeches include Ann Coulter, Henry Kissinger, Charlton Heston, and Condoleezza Rice.

What is the reason for this backlash? Within three minutes of a speech by Gavin McInnes in February 2017, the New York City Police had to be called to the New York University campus. How is hearing an opposing viewpoint physically dangerous? College age students, remember, have been raised in the modern age of child-centered philosophy. Everyone gets a trophy and there are no losers. In my son's conservative soccer league, for example, all the children receive participation awards. Each child is guaranteed to be a winner. After complaints, the coach reported that he tried to end this practice but the outcry from conservative parents was too great.

Today's children, in general, are survivors of divorce or abandonment. Their family lives had been often touched by some sort of dysfunction: sexual, physical or substance abuse. Many of these children have grown up and are now college age. (They also take a lot of selfies.) As seen in music lyrics and in popular kids shows, parents are portrayed as irresponsible people who pay little attention to their kids beyond their own personal problems.

University college students are also the byproducts of the Progressive Education movement. Hallmark of this movement is the removal of anything remotely connected to absolute truth; the Ten Commandments and other Bible readings/prayers were thrown out public schools in 1960. Situational ethics concealed under the ruse of "cultural sensitivity" became the classroom norm. Christmas trees became Holiday Trees and the Gender Spectrum was introduced in Health class. Common Core Standards were introduced, and some Liberal teachers encouraged their young students to sing praise songs to President Obama.

Children were forcibly fed a liberal diet of tolerance, gun control, climate change and called their teachers, "Friends."

Educational policies have existed in American public schools for at least a decade. Children's games such as Musical Chairs and Duck, Duck Goose were no longer encouraged in school because they were mean-spirited and harmful. While in a pedagogy development class in Teacher College, a Yale curriculum developer spoke to my class openly about the underlying goal of Situational Ethics, commonplace in the 90s. Situational Ethics, or study of differing cultural norms, was designed to teach the children that there is **no such thing as an absolute**. What is right in one culture is not right in another. Who decides which norm is correct? The people within that society!

University professors also contribute to the spread of Liberalism on college campuses. According to a 2008 study, The Liberal (and Moderating) Professoriate, by Scott Jaschik, based on a study of 1,417 full-time, college professors, 46.1% categorized themselves as Moderates, 44.1% categorized themselves as Liberals and 9.2% categorized themselves as Conservatives. In Liberal Arts colleges, the differential is greater: 61% identify as

Liberals and 3.9% identify as Some Liberal professors have even initiated campus protests, staged classroom walkouts or participated in violence themselves.

A few professors have supported Antifa, the anti fascist movement whose mission is, according to their website, *"to drive out the Trump/Pence regime,"* in the name of humanity. Mark Bray, a professor at Dartmouth College, published The Antifascist Handbook, that he describes as an *"unabashedly partisan call to arms."* Professor George Ciccariello, from Drexel University tweeted to his students on Twitter, *"All I want for Christmas is White Genocide,"* on Christmas Eve, 2016. If college professors are acting this way, it is reasonable to expect some of their students will follow in their footsteps.

Back on campus, the children "who never lost" for the first time have encountered opposing viewpoints. With the recent campus derangement, there has been the rise of Campus Safe Spaces. These are areas that are "safe environments," free from criticism, harassment, and macroaggression. Safe spaces are havens for the sexually assaulted, transgender, LGBT students or anyone in need of a hug. Safe spaces provide cookies, calming music, therapy animal (real or plush), Play Doh and show videos of frolicking puppies. One campus, the University of East

Anglia, outlawed sombreros in a Mexican student restaurant because of fears of triggering trauma in students. Students have been observed sobbing, shrieking and hugging during Far-Right speaking events. This student reaction is extreme considering that they are not forced to attend the speeches, but object to their existence in their proximity.

A significant rise in rage expressed on American college and university campuses has been observed since the election of President Donald Trump in 2017. Timothy Tia, a student from the University of Florida, said to the Huffington Post that Far Right speakers *"have to be considered a serious threat to this country. They are white supremacists, after all, who want to take power. It might be unthinkable now, but it was unthinkable two years ago that someone as divisive and offensive as Donald Trump would become president."*

Donald Trump is not a white supremacist; he has worked hard to bring about change and reform for all Americans. The 2018 record-low unemployment numbers for African Americans (6.8%) and Hispanics (4.9%) attest to that. He usually, however, gets a mention each time the Far Right is concerned. Why? Is this Trump Derangement Syndrome again?

A recent study concluded that parents who put their children on a pedestal and showered them with praise were likely to plant the seeds of narcissism at an early age. University of Amsterdam psychologist, Eddie Brummelman and his team in 2015 from the Netherlands studied more than 565 children for several years. They found that children who had been "overvalued" by their parents were more likely to suffer from narcissism. The Brummelman Team asked families to complete detailed questionnaires that assessed narcissistic development. Questions asked of participants included whether or not they agreed with statements such as *"kids like me deserve something extra"*. Their parents were asked to judge whether their child was *"more special than other children,"* a measure of whether they overvalued their children.

Dr Brummelman theorized that when children are seen by their parents as being more special and more entitled than other children, they were likely to internalize the view that they are superior individuals. This is the core tenet of narcissism. It is no small wonder that such a culture would encourage narcissistic development.

Interestingly, while it might seem likely that a child narcissist is the product of narcissistic parents, the researchers found no evidence for this. Nor did they find a lack of parental warmth and affection was linked to narcissism, as some previous studies have postulated. Problems with Narcissism, according to the Mayo Clinic, seem to arise when parents are "poorly attuned with their child's experience." Self-regulation is problematic at best.

When the overly-praised, narcissist develops into a college -aged student, rage occurs when special treatment and endless affirmation fails to take place. No doubt, by their own admission, students feel threatened by President Trump, but their problems began decades before his election in 2017.

www.mayoclinic.org/diseases-conditions/narcissistic-perso nality-disorder/symptoms-causes/syc-20366662

Eddie Brummelman, Sander Thomaes, Stefanie A. Nelemans, Bram Orobio de Castro, Geertjan Overbeek, and Brad J.Bushman, *Origins of Narcissism in Children*, PNAS, March 24, 2015

Katy Steinmetz, "Milo Yiannopoulos Finally Spoke at Berkeley. But the Protesters Were Louder," *Time Magazine*, September 25, 2017 Durden, Tyler, Meet Six College Professors Who Promote Violence, Zero Hedge, October 13, 2017

Chapter 6
Fantasy

Narcissists are generally preoccupied with some sort of fantasy. Their "visions" mostly center around their personal success or the effectiveness of a cause or project. Their daydreams can be heroic, hostile, sexual, or achievement oriented. They also use fantasy to cope with stress. Entitled, they exaggerate their stories to make themselves feel even more superior to those around them, weaving a self-love mythology as they go. Their storytelling gives them breath; it gives them wings. The philosopher, Rene Descartes, said, *"I think; therefore, I am."* The narcissist says, *"I have drama; therefore, I am significant."*

Who doesn't love a good story? It begins with an epic conflict where the destiny of all that is just and good hangs in the balance. The Evil Villain is hell-bent on destroying the main characters. Just when all seems frantically lost, a hero rides in on his white horse to save the day. He gets the girl, humanity is saved, and everyone lives happily-ever-after. The hero also gets a victory march with a tear-stained audience gratefully applauding him.

The Climate Change and Global Warming narrative provides the perfect storybook backdrop for many Democrat and Liberal activists. Here, leaders (and pundits) lead a noble crusade to save the planet and a mankind from the harmful effects of pollution and greenhouse gases. The situation is dire. Mankind is not expected to survive for long if something doesn't happen quickly. As ice caps melt and polar bears drown, the Climate Change hero, Al Gore appears upon his white, carbon-emitting, Cessna jet. Already married to Princess Tipper, he leaps to the podium to save humanity, one speech at a time.

Mid-speech the villain, President Donald J. Trump enters the scene. He rips up the Paris Climate Agreement signed by President Obama in 2015 (which was never sanctioned by the US Congress. Snap!) 195 countries had adopted this first-ever, legally binding global climate deal in Paris, France. It imposed sanctions on countries that did not take measures to limit carbon emissions/pollution. It promised to rid the planet from the evil nemesis: the consumption of fossil fuels! Countries could now no longer work together in a spirit of global unity and harmony. Trump was clearly trying to destroy the world and everyone living in it!!!

When President Trump pulled the United States out of the Paris Climate Agreement, on June 1, 2017, the global activists suffered from full blown fits of Trump Derangement Syndrome. The planet was in mortal danger and President Trump received international criticism. All seemed lost, even though meteorologists had only been collecting data on the earth's climate for a short period of time: 100 years. Severe storms came that confirmed all fears, even though National Weather Service only began collecting weather data in 1947 (But don't let that ruin the story.) The end was near. Barack Obama, eco warrior of the Climate Change saga, did not even get his victory march!

With the election of Donald Trump spoiled everything, things changed. World leaders agreed. Obama called it, *"the urgent threat of a changing climate."* Jim Yong Kim, President of the World Bank said, *"We have to wake up to the fierce urgency of now."* French President, Emmanuel Macron tweeted, "it's a mistake for our planet. Climate change is already changing our daily lives. It's not the future we want for our world." He later scolded Climate Change naysayers in a speech saying, *"To all the scientists, engineers, entrepreneurs, and responsible citizens who were disappointed by the decision by the president of the United States, I want to say they will find* in France a second homeland. I call on them — come and work here with us, to work together on concrete solutions for our climate."

California Climate Change activist, Mr. K., gives the activist perspective in his apocalyptic rant in the Ukiah Daily Journal: *"Meanwhile, Trump is hell bent on destroying Obama's legacy, including eviscerating the EPA, which has removed climate change information from its web site. You may already be aware of the importance of addressing global warming. The real problem is: too many people using too many resources, at too fast a rate. It's simply unsustainable. When the human race finally discovers that our survival is on the line, some things will have to change. When arid land no longer supports enough crops to feed everybody and there's a shortage of potable water, it will already be too late for hundreds of millions. To say nothing of the conflicts those shortages will ignite? What will happen when Himalayan glacial melt water that supplies nuclear armed China, India and Pakistan starts to dry up? Eventually, a shortage of resources will mandate practicing conservation and thrift, with a focus on using sustainable resources. Will it be too little, too late?"*

Steven Hawkings, a well-known physicist also agreed that humanity was at a "tipping point" where global warming would become so dangerous that earth would *"become like Venus, with a temperature of 250 degrees Celsius, and raining sulfuric acid."* The only logical answer to the catastrophe for Hawkings was to leave earth as soon as possible. He warned, *"If humans don't become a multi-planetary species and settle on other worlds, our species could die out within the next century."* In other words, humans needed to board spacecrafts ASAP to repopulate the universe. He made another sensational prediction that Artificial Intelligence would ultimately become the new life form to replace humans, in a CNBC report. Robots would rule the world.

The entire Hawkings, end-of-the-world scenario is somewhat reminiscent of a 1950s Sci-Fi movie. Climate Change Activists, however, continue to take the doomsday threat seriously. Since President Trump, the environmental nemesis, has scuttled humanity, many are now frantically working out their escape plans to move to Mars in 2025. It exists. Mars One is a 6-million-dollar project (at this point) whose goal is: *"to establish a permanent human settlement on Mars. Mars is the only planet we know of that can currently feasibly support human life and will be humankind's first step to become a multiplanetary species. Before carefully selected and trained crews will depart to Mars, several unmanned missions will be completed, establishing a habitable settlement waiting for the first astronauts to arrive. The Mars One crews will go to Mars not to simply visit, but to live, explore, and create a second home for humanity. The first men and women to go to Mars are going there to stay."*

Never doubt that a Climate Change activist takes advocacy or militancy lightly. Climate Change activism is a good indicator of what degree an individual is engaged in Democratic Liberalism. There are many degrees of activism which correspond to the commitment level to environmental causes. The common denominator, however, is that President Trump and his conservative cronies are out to destroy the world and that it is up to caring Democratic Liberals to save humanity.

The narcissist creates a narrative to gain significance. What could be more significant than saving the world? The Climate Change movement is a convenient vehicle for many narcissistic Liberals to express themselves. If the narrative is contradicted in any way, derangement results. No one wants to die, but do these people really believe they are going to die? Perhaps working this narrative can help some Democratic narcissists relieve election loss stress and provide them with distraction from the Obama executive mandate reversals.

----

http://www.ukiahdailyjournal.com/article/NP/20170716/LCAL1/170719930

https://www.ncbi.nlm.nih.gov/pubmed/1939692

https://www.weforum.org/agenda/2015/11/15-quotes-on-climate-change-by-world-leaders/

http://www.newsweek.com/stephen-hawking-end-year-predictions-2017-755952 https://www.mars-one.com/

Chapter 7
Gaslighting

Narcissists, in general, tend to sacrifice their victims on the altar of their own self-love. They have little to no regard for their feelings and interests of their significant other. They lack emotional empathy (not intellectual- they know what they are doing) and their relationships are not long lasting. Because of their need for excessive attention, emotionally secure people typically avoid them.

Narcissists are frequently abusive. A narcissist will abuse by demanding another person to give up who they are. They do this to increase their personal power. Sometimes, the narcissist will manipulate their victim so badly, the person will question their own sanity or reality. When this technique occurs, usually by means of verbal and psychological abuse, it is called "gaslighting."

The term "gaslighting" originated from the 1944 movie, Gaslight. where a man manipulates his wife to believe that she is crazy. He adjusts the gaslights in his home and when his wife notices the change, he accuses her of being at first inaccurate. He was trying to cover up a murder and succeeded in making poor Ingrid Bergman believe that **she** was, in fact, the problem. It is a horrible story of psychological abuse directed towards someone who was supposed to be loved.

Look at this face. Look into this young woman's eyes. This is a photo of my beautiful mother, Mary Agnes. She was a wonderful person. She was bubbly, fun, and the type of person that everyone told their problems to. She was ahead of her time because she insisted on attending college when most girls her age married after high school.

Mom wanted to see the world, so after graduating from college, she applied to work at the State Department as a secretary. She attended most of the post-World War II conferences and even had her picture on the cover of Life magazine (she was going to work at the Berlin Conference in 1954).

Independent, pretty and intelligent, she worked by day and waltzed with diplomats by night. She worked for notables such as John Foster Dulles (Dulles Airport in Washington, DC is named after him) and Richard Nixon when he was Vice-President under Dwight Eisenhower. (Mom was friends with all the Watergate secretaries and knew Rosemary Woods personally. In fact, my mom was a human listening device for Nixon because mechanical listening devices had been invented yet. In those days, it was common for secretaries to routinely listen into important conversations and take notes in shorthand. Mom used to help Nixon keep appointments and micromanage important executive details.)

Around 1960, Mom realized that if she continued to work for Mr. Nixon, she would be a spinster. She described Richard Nixon as a micromanager. She loved her boss, but he demanded 24/7 commitment from his staff. Her biological clock was ticking. Mom left her job and began looking for a husband to settle down to raise a family. There was a problem with that, however; most eligible men were either already married or had been killed in World War II. Mom also had standards. She wanted a comfortable life, children, a nice home and a country club. She wasn't going to marry just anybody.

Mom met Dad in a reception line at her local Catholic church. Dad was dashing, intelligent, handsome and-most importantly- available! He seemed to be from a good family, had a great job in the Department of Justice. He was working on a master's degree at American University. What was not to like? They became an item almost immediately.

There was a tragic flaw, however, in the love story: Dad suffered from Narcissist Personality Disorder. He was also bipolar. Dad's condition was never officially diagnosed. Because he was such an intelligent manipulator, he managed to evade professional intervention for decades. Look again at the picture of my mother. This is the face of a gaslighting victim. She died of a broken heart at age 67 after decades of personal misery and verbal abuse. I had a front row seat to this tragedy along with my younger brother.

How did such an intelligent and lovely person fall victim to such psychological abuse? There are identifiable characteristics to narcissistic gaslighting. Hopefully, when the following red flags are raised and recognized, future unsuspecting victims can be spared or encouraged to escape.

Step One: The Bait

No one signs up in a relationship with a narcissist to be gaslighted or abused. How does the Narcissist attract his or her victims? Misery loves company, and the narcissist must be validated in his self-deluding world. In addition, the narcissist always demands the best mate; he or she wants the most attractive and intelligent because, after all, they deserve the very best. It takes much work to attract the very best.
They begin by drowning the potential partners in praise. A narcissist pours it on thick. He or she will assure their victims that they are the most desirable person on the planet. There has never been anyone born who is as wonderful. This praise will mirror the self-praise of the narcissist in intensity. The relationship must be destined because the two are a perfect, superhuman match.

Mom recounted that when she first met my father, she had been head-over-heels, swept off her feet. Their relationship was immediately intense. He flooded her with his attention. She also said that Dad did all the talking and most of the conversation centered around him. Red flag?

Step 2: Ghosting

A tactic that narcissist will use once a relationship has established is emotional ghosting. Bankrupt of empathy, the narcissist will test the validity of the new emotional attachment. One day, the narcissist will be the caring, best friend. The next day, all emotional support suddenly disappears. The stunned victim then seeks to re-establish the lost emotional connection. The narcissist returns only to later cut the victim off emotionally again. This pattern repeats back and forth, in an unreliable and unpredictable manner, very much like the appearance and disappearance of a ghost. This is especially painful if the victim enjoyed the previous praise and sell job that the narcissist had performed to win her (or him) in the first place.

My mother had many physical ailments throughout her life. One condition that she suffered greatly from daily was rheumatoid arthritis. Dad narrowly showed compassion through difficult tasks; mom was forced to carry the groceries, keep the house and hold down a job and was accused daily of being lazy when she could not physically keep up. At times, he would help her, particularly after a surgery or to avoid hiring a nurse to save money.

More often, however, compassion would disappear in ghost-like manner. Once, when Mom had broken her wrist in a serious fall and confined to bed, she became hungry. Dad threw an orange at her to eat. She could not peel it because of her cast. He congratulated himself for his charity and criticized her for not being grateful for his gift.

Step 3: Abusive Criticism

After the narcissist has completely secured his victim, abuse will begin. It usually begins with verbal abuse. The narcissist belittles his partner without mercy. Because he has a need to feel superior, he must put this person down. This abuse is evidence of a narcissist's smokescreen to hide a fragile self-image or personal shortcomings. The devil is said to be in the details. The narcissist will attack the little things the victim does: how they wear their clothes, their beliefs, opinions, how they brush their teeth. No territory is spared.

After the gaslighting, the victim of the narcissist first learns to question him or herself. He questions if he or she simply can do anything the right way. These are the first indicators that the gaslighting has been effective. The victim believe that what the narcissist says about them is the truth. He or she probably is stupid, lazy, inconsiderate, selfish… the list is long.

The narcissist directs verbal assault in the gaslighting process beyond personal introspection. The focus shifts from self-doubt to belief that ***everyone around me also thinks that I am an idiot or a loser.*** The narcissist subjugates his victim this way. The vicious, slanderous and invented accusations are now believed by the victim to be global. First, the warped, self-poison is fed. Then, upon digestion, the lies are projected externally. Gaslighting has proved to the victim that the falsehoods are now universally accepted truth. Reality has changed; victory is complete. "IF everybody knew what I knew about you…" is often what I would hear my Dad say.

Step 4: Rage

Inevitably, narcissistic abuse segways into narcissistic rage. The victim naturally does not want at first to put up with abuse. He or she must be beaten into submission. My mother told the story of her first beating by the hands of my father. It happened on the night of the assassination of President John F. Kennedy, November 22, 1963. My parents had been married for almost two years. I was a little over a year old. Mom, pregnant with my younger brother, was concerned about my Dad. He regularly fought with his co-workers in the office. She made him a nice dinner to provide a bit of escape for the upsetting news coverage of the assassination.

When Dad saw the dinner, there was an outburst of rage. Not only did Dad destroy the dinner by smashing it around their DC apartment, he smashed his pregnant wife as well. Mom was covered in black and blue marks because she had been disrespectful to the President Kennedy's memory. Mom told her horrified father that she had fallen down the stairs.

Step 5: Changing Reality

Again, to manipulate effectively, the narcissist will use any means necessary to insure the complete subjugation and dependence of his or her victim. This is achieved by gaslighting or altering the perception of the person the abuse is directed towards. As previously stated, the narcissist deluges his victim with a torrent of lies- usually via personal attack. Then, abuse becomes directed towards an individual in a group- many times the abused person's family members. Rage first wears out the victim so that he willingly accepts that he is_____ (fill in the blank: stupid, ugly, a whore, etc.), then it scares the victim into believing everyone else agrees with warped reality. Rage is the catalyst of gaslighting; it facilitates the smooth transition of power to the evil dictator.

Look again at my Mom's adorable, Irish face. She travelled the world working for important people. She volunteered in a local charity. My Dad, however, wanted to keep her under control by expressing rage. Mom was perfectly capable of divorcing Dad and supporting us children. Divorce, however, for many was a unknown option in the 1970s. Furthermore, Catholic girls did not divorce. Cultural norms, therefore, worked against her release from the bondage of Narcissism.

Dad had to work overtime expressing rage, but ultimately succeeded in making my mother believe that divorce was impossible. He threatened daily that he would never pay support if she left. He added this accusation to the daily litany of her personal failures. It weighed her down. Sometimes, after a severe rage, Dad would make up for it, aware that he had again crossed a terrible line. He would be a sorry but then ghost-out emotionally in less than 48 hours. There was always some justification to his fits of rage. It was hard to keep up. His excuses left us all mentally exhausted.

How did this gaslighting experience end for my Mom? Although she stayed with my Dad, Mom turned to alcohol. She died too early in life. Be not deceived. Gaslighting abuse will take a person out. If you suspect that you are in a gaslighting relationship- RUN! You cannot fix this person. This fix requires extreme measures and professional help. If you have already been worn out by abuse, it is difficult to find the energy to cope, let alone fight back. Mom died three years after Dad retired from working for the federal government. Retirement brought on full-time misery.

One note of victory in Mom's life, however, was that she never believed that she was stupid. She did admit freely that she had made a stupid choice in marrying Dad, but never gave up that she had skills. Although she depended on alcohol, she limited her drinking only to when Dad was in the house. Once I was married, her physical health declined quickly. After Dad's retirement, Mom escaped the home by volunteering as a support provider in hospital waiting rooms. Mom loved life and wanted grandchildren. One day, she will be able to meet them.

The Point

Gaslighting is evil and it does not require rocket science to recognize its devastating effects. The hard lessons of gaslighting for family members are not easily forgotten. Survivors readily recognize narcissism when the ugly head rears up in different people, groups and circumstances.

Chapter 8
Mainstream Media Gaslighting

Reality changed greatly for many Liberals and Democrats on the night of November 8, 2016. Hillary Clinton had failed to break the glass ceiling. Donald Trump won Pennsylvania, then North Carolina, Florida...until he won the entire Electoral College in a landslide. Clinton supporters were distraught, crying and rolling around on the floor. How could this have happened?

The Mainstream Media has been unapologetic in their hatred for Donald Trump. Pre-election, they reported daily that it was absolutely and completely impossible, based on polling numbers, for President Trump to win. Many laughed and sneered that he considered it reasonable to run for the office of President in the first place. They tried to pin scandals to him, such as Trump's locker room banter (caught on tape about a female reporter), tax evasion, shady property deals and his use of bankruptcy laws. Nothing seemed to stick.

Then, Donald Trump won the White House. The Mainstream Media consists of TV news outlets such as CNN, MSNBC, Public Television, ABC, CBS, and the BBC. Newspapers that align themselves as mainstream are numerous and include: The New York Times, The Washington Post, The Baltimore Sun and the Associated Press. Like-minded, online digital and/or entertainment content include BuzzFeed, the Huffington Post, and Mashable and BoredPanda. Social Media outlets like Facebook and Twitter also are boldly left-leaning when promoting algorithms or digital content. Together, these organizations combined to become the Mainstream Media or the Leftist Groupthink of the 21st century.

There are many parallels that exist between gaslighting narcissists and the Mainstream Media as it seeks to bring change into American society. The steps of their gaslighting process on their public audiences are identical. Gaslighting is the number one tool used by modern and upset Democratic Liberals. Trump Derangement Syndrome, if anything, is the greatest indicator that such abuse is taking place. Do you enjoy being gaslit from the comfort of your viewing couch?

Step One: The Bait

The Mainstream Media lures its audience with bait- Click Bait to be exact. Click Bait can be many things that internet surfers want to "click on" while surfing online waves. It can be an adorable video of baby animals or the antics of a toddler. It can be an interesting human interest story or a survey to determine your Elf Name. More often, it is a shocking story of gossip, betrayal or bizarre relationship that went wrong. No matter what the Click Bait is, the goal is the same: get the online web-goer to click on the story and sell advertising.

BuzzFeed, for example, is an expert on providing its viewers Click Bait. This news and online media organization uploads a wide range of entertainment sources to online media goers. Although profits are recently down, this company made $170 million in 2015 and had, for example, 800,000 people simultaneously tune in to watch a watermelon explode in April 2016. Fun and non-threatening entertainment is just a click away- unless, of course, you are the watermelon.

The Democratic Party, from its party platform, Change That Matters, also advertises positive slogans and campaign promises to attract new members. It promises many things: raising worker wages, protecting workers rights, supporting working families, expanding affordable housing, ensuring retirement, ending racism, guaranteeing rights of women, transgenders and the LGBTQ community, securing climate justice, universal health care, ending gun violence, and much more. They claim that they are the friend of not only the hard worker, but the marginalized, the discriminated against and the downtrodden.

Who wouldn't want to help people like the Democratic Party? While advertising, they portray Republicans as money-hungry capitalists who neither care for the poor and the needy or try to protect their rights. Inherently inserted is the idea that the person **needs** the party in order to survive in a dangerous Republican environment. The bait works. Co-dependency is initiated.

https://www.democrats.org/party-platform

Step Two: Ghosting

Democrats, after flooding prospective members with pledges and cultivating co-dependence, engage in random ghosting. The Mainstream Media co-ghosts leftist associates with their coverage- or lack of coverage-of political issues. Once their audience is emotionally committed, Democrats and media counterparts suddenly disappear from the progressive scene. One example of a group that has suffered from this tactic has been the DACA children; the sons and daughters of illegal immigrants who were brought to America as small children.

Under the Deferred Action for Childhood Arrivals program, deportation is delayed for two-year, renewable time periods and the recipients during those times become eligible for work permits. President Obama further promised such children in June 2012, a path to citizenship under the Dream Act policy and accepted applications. The future looked bright for these Dreamers as Democrats championed this cause and protected behind their humanitarian shields. The Mainstream Media faithfully brought this story to public attention, highlighting the plight and saga of the children. Suddenly, however, the

Democrats and their media co-ghosts vanished mysteriously off TV sets in their support of the DACA children.

Where had they gone? Were they floating, eerily disembodied over the Capitol building? No, they simply did not approve of President Trump's plan concerning the DACA children and refused to negotiate with him on the children's behalf. Mainstream media coverage went silent. President Trump tweeted: *"Cannot believe how BADLY DACA recipients have been treated by the Democrats...totally abandoned! Republicans are still working hard,"* on February 16, 2018.

DACA had been, previous to this tweet, under review by the Department of Homeland Security. The Expansion of this program had earlier that June. When 700,000 illegal children started pouring over the Mexican border during that year **without parents**- to take advantage of the DACA program, President Trump was forced to take action. He put forward plans to phase out the program under certain conditions: the ending of the visa lottery program, the limiting of chain migration and the provision of funding for a border wall. In exchange for these conditions, President Trump promised to extend protection to 1.8 immigrants.

Senator Ted Cruz stated, "*President Trump's immigration proposal is more liberal than former President Obama's Deferred Action for Childhood Arrivals (DACA) program…DACA covered 690,000 people, why on earth are Republicans trying to more than double, nearly triple that?*" News reporters declined to comment further on DACA issues under this Democratic ghosting. This is not an uncommon pattern for both groups; the Democratic leadership ghosts and the Mainstream Media follows this leading.

http://thehill.com/homenews/senate/373995-cruz-trumps-immigration-proposal-is-more-liberal-than-obamas

After offering the deal, President Trump waited in the Oval Office for Democrats to approve in the Congress his DACA proposition that advocated American security and vetting of children- often MS 16 gang member/recruits- as they surged over the southern border. His pen was ready to sign the legislation into law. The Democrats were strangely silent. 1.8 million immigrants were left unprocessed-wondering what would happen to them next.

No DACA agreement has since been reached or proposed by Congress since President Trump's proposal. Where did everybody go? Dreamer, Hilario Yanez stated, *"As far as the Democrats, I'm a little confused as to what their message is. I'm a little confused as to what they believe in."* Ghostbusters reported much paranormal activity that day on the grounds of Capitol Hill.

News media ghosting haunted the 2017 media coverage of the Baltimore City Public School System in Baltimore, Maryland. Phantom Democratic Leadership, along with The Baltimore Sun newspaper, spearheaded The Maryland Educational Trust Fund initiative which built six casinos to fund the public-school education of Maryland's children. Advertised heavily before elections, these casinos were heralded as great opportunities to bring millions of dollars to educate the children. The casinos did produce these funds, pumping 1.7 billion dollars into the educational trust. Over time, however, casino funds were noticeable absent from the school budgets. Baltimore City schools had- incredibly- experienced funding cuts. Talk was big in Baltimore while three casinos were under construction.

Baltimore City leaders and media coverage of promised casino-school funding soon went missing in action post construction. Two years later, during the bitter winter of 2018, a crisis faced public schools in Baltimore City. It began on January 4, 2018, when schools were closed for two days due to lack of heat. One-third (sixty) of Baltimore City schools housed decrepit furnaces that required major repairs. A heating crisis resulted. Could not the casino funds helped with this problem to fix the furnaces?

Children shivered in their classrooms, wearing coats and gloves, huddled around space heaters brought into the school by concerned parents. Preschoolers cried on the news from their classrooms. Decrepit school buildings showed little signs of improvement. Fighting deadlines and state regulations (initiated by failed Democratic policies) to prevent waste, Baltimore City was forced to return $66 million dollars back to the State of Maryland, delaying or outright halting school repairs until a future time.

The mayor of Baltimore, Catherine Pugh, however, was able to allocate city funds to the support of undocumented immigrants, establishing Baltimore as a Sanctuary City. (Pugh prefers to call Baltimore a "Welcoming City.") She allocated $200,000 dollars to provide illegal aliens free legal defense from federal deportation lawyers. Later in the year, Mayor Pugh approved $100,000 to hire a fleet of buses to transport students to attend "A March for Our Lives," a planned national gun protest in Washington, DC., on March 24, 2018. What??? Clearly, it would be expected that Democrat Mayor Pugh would endorse Democratic/Liberal causes, but for heaven's sake, fix the school buildings first! It seemed the city leaders and the MSM certainly lacked in school spirit- pun intended.

On a national level, severe weather event news coverages are further examples of nationwide media ghosting. In 2017, Harvey, Irma and Maria devastated the Caribbean, Florida and Texas. Newscasters covered each storm in detail as it made landfall and ravaged property. Wind speeds, storm paths and storm surges were updated hourly. Death counts were tallied and survivor stories retold. Relief efforts were covered for about a week. Then, as with previous storms, the Mainstream Media vanished suddenly as new stories came and went. Storm victims were abandoned as they pieced their lives back together again. Each hurricane season tracks a similar ghosting MSM pattern.

http://www.baltimoresun.com/news/maryland/education/bs-md-ci-western-high-school-cold-20171214-story.html
http://thehill.com/homenews/senate/373995-cruz-trumps-immigration-proposal-is-more-liberal-than-obamas
https://www.citylab.com/equity/2018/01/how-baltimore-students-got-left-in-the-cold/549866/

http://www.baltimoresun.com/news/maryland/education/bs-md-ci-schools-money-returned-20180104-story.h

http://www.baltimoresun.com/news/maryland/baltimore-city/bs-md-ci-deportation-lawyers-20180306-story.html

Step Three: Abusive Criticism

BuzzFeed, however, like many digital content organizations, beyond its Click Bait, also provides current events or mainstream news stories to their readers. Link to link, the coverage is overwhelmingly negative towards Conservatives to criticise them. President Donald J. Trump, for example, has often been targeted in negative reports, even though he is a moderate conservative.

In the Pew Research Center Study of 2017, researchers studied news stories of for the first sixty days of the Trump Administration. The study analyzed content from national newspaper websites, radio, cable and network broadcasts, websites, and digital outlets reporting about President Trump from January 21st through April 30th, 2017. Two-thirds of newscaster statements were negative concerning President Trump, "more than twice the negativity seen in stories from the first 60 days of Bill Clinton, George W. Bush or Barack Obama's presidencies. Only 5% of statements were positive, compared to 42% of stories reported on President Obama. The percentages tallied in 2018 have been roughly the same.

The Mainstream News Media clearly harbors a bias against President Trump. According to Student News Daily, 39% of news coverage was focused on Trump scandals, 45% of negative press was directed at Trump's policies and the remaining airtime was spent criticizing Trump's top officials. As more Democratic or Liberal accomplishments are overturned by President Trump, the more abusive criticism becomes.

https://www.npr.org/2017/10/02/555092743/study-news-coverage-of-trump-more-negative-than-for-other-presidents
http://www.journalism.org/2017/10/02/covering-president-trump-in-a-polarized-media-environment/
https://www.studentnewsdaily.com/example-of-media-bias/90-negative-coverage-of-trump-in-the-media-leads-to-increased-approval-rating/

The narcissist chooses his target and verbally assaults him relentlessly. He beats down this person down until submission is absolute. President Trump is not alone to receive verbal assault in news coverage. No one is safe, even if their performance record is stellar.

Navy Rear Admiral Ronny Jackson, for example, served as the White House doctor under three presidential administrations: Presidents George Bush, Barack Obama and Donald Trump. Former senior advisor to President Obama, Dan Pfeiffer, stated, *"Dr. Jackson is a phenomenal doctor and a really great guy. He and his team took great care of all of us for many years."* He was called a "saint" and a "phenomenal doctor." Obama himself called Jackson, "A most impressive leader." Jackson had maintained a distinguished service record since 1995. All was going well for Dr. Jackson until President Trump chose him to be the Secretary of Veterans Affairs. For this crime, (and possibly for affirming that President Trump was mentally fit) the Mainstream Media set out to assassinate Dr. Jackson's character in to coerce him to resign from this nomination.

Accusations, originating from disgruntled co-worker, Dr. Jennifer Pena (doctor to Vice-President Pence) and Democratic Senator from Montana, Jon Tester, spewed forth in a merciless smear campaign against Dr. Jackson. Refusing to identify his sources, Tester affirmed that Dr. Jackson, in a CNN interview with Anderson Cooper in April 2018, *"He handed out prescription drugs like they were candy."* Dr. Jackson, who some staffers, according to Tester, called "the Candyman," was frequently drunk on duty while President Obama was in his care. Also, according to Tester, Jackson drunkenly banged on the doors of female employee during an overseas trip, wrecked a government car, prescribed opiates to himself and another White House staffer, and oversaw a hostile work environment.

Does this make sense? Security surrounding the President of the United States is tight. Medicines are strictly controlled and monitored. Secret Service agents surround the President 24/7. Is it likely that no one noticed such strange behavior and that it went unreported for three administrations?

Even CNN was embarrassed by this smear campaign which was remarkably lacking in credible witnesses. Scott Jennings from CNN wrote: *"The shameful smearing of Dr. Ronny Jackson, House physician who was nominated by President Donald Trump to be Secretary of the Veterans Affairs Administration and has now withdrawn, is example*

#967 of why people hate Washington D.C. and were in a revolutionary mood at the 2016 ballot box. Montana Senator Jon Tester, in particular ought to be ashamed of publicly airing unproven allegations against a Navy Admiral and doctor who has served his nation and three Commanders-in-Chief with honor. Tester sullied the reputation of a good man and no doubt chilled many people who ever had a fleeting thought of offering themselves up for public service."

Jackson denied the false allegations saying: *"The allegations against me are completely false and fabricated. If they had any merit, I would have not been selected, promoted and entrusted to serve in such a sensitive and important role as physician to three presidents over the past 12 years."* Jackson resigned stating, *"these false allegations have become a distraction for this President and the important issue we must be addressing-how we give the best care to our nation's heroes. While I will be forever grateful for the trust and confidence President Trump has placed in me by giving me this opportunity, I am regretfully withdrawing my nomination to be Secretary for the Department of Veteran Affairs."*

https://nypost.com/2018/04/26/ronny-jackson-withdraws-a
s-va-secretary-nominee/

This character attack on a great American servant, Dr. Ronny Jackson was brazenly abusive. Of course, a doctor gives out medication. When traveling through time zones, sleeping aides are regularly prescribed to negate the effects of jet lag. (How important is it to be alert on an official presidential visit on so many levels? Very!!) Dr. Jackson never wrecked a car and the Secret Service disputed the allegations against him. The Mainstream Media, however, blasted these allegations across headlines, insinuating that President Trump picked inferior people for cabinet positions. Johnson is not the only Trump appointee to be smeared. Betsy Devos (Department of Education), Mike Pompeo (Secretary of State), and Gina Haspel (Central Intelligence Agency) have also found themselves in these crosshairs of cruelty.

According to Press Secretary, Sarah Huckabee Sanders, *"43% of Trump's nominations are still awaiting confirmation in the Senate."* President Trump tweeted on March 11, 2018: *"The Democrats continue to Obstruct the confirmation of hundreds of good and talented people who are needed to run our government...A record in U.S.*

*history. State Department, Ambassadors and many others
are being slow walked. Senate must approve NOW!"*

Democratic Liberals, enabled by the Mainstream Media,
have verbally abused many great, American servants. The
goal of this abuse is to control dissidents or those who
dare oppose their chosen political agenda or movement.

http://thehill.com/homenews/administration/377829-trump-
hits-dems-on-record-number-of-unconfirmed-nominees
https://www.youtube.com/watch?v=_beA5vPkjdA
https://www.cnn.com/2018/04/30/politics/karen-pence-doct
or-privacy-ronny-jackson/index.html
https://www.cnn.com/2018/04/30/opinions/smearing-of-ron
ny-jackson-tester-is-shameful-jennings-opinion/index.html
http://www.businessinsider.com/obama-officials-praise-whi
te-house-doctor-trump-physical-2018-1

Step 4: Rage

Expressions of rage, associated with Trump Derangement
Syndrome and Democratic Leaders on Capitol Hill, are
broadcasted daily throughout Mainstream Media news
coverage. **Rage is used by them as an effective tool,
by Narcissists to control individuals and/or people
groups.** Rage expressions, in much the same way,

regularly and intentionally facilitate the advancement of Democratic and Liberal agenda. One Democratic Senator, Cory Booker (aka "I Am Spartacus") has been particularly loud, recently screaming, *"I am frankly seething with anger… (and) had tears of rage,"* over vulgar comments President Trump had allegedly concerning African nations. He yelled at Kirstjen Nielsen, *"tens of millions of Americans are hurting right now because of what they're worried about what happened in the White House, that's unacceptable to me!"*

Outbursts of Democrat rage are regularly televised on news channels; tune in to the daily White House Press Briefing for daily proof.

A Rage Campaign occurs when many rage expressions are channeled to catalyze political agenda. The average Rage Campaign last approximately one week in the Mainstream Media. Rage topics include DACA funding, Climate Change, the separation of families illegally entering the USA at the border, porn star payments and the confirmation of new Supreme Court Justices. Once the one week mark has passed, a new rage campaigns is fabricated or highlighted to replace it. It is not always clear if the intended goal of the Rage Campaign is covert or directed. It mirrors political campaigns in that the only acceptable outcome is winning. The Rage Campaign, however, is highly efficient means to wear out listening TV audiences into accepting new norms of behavior or Democratic/Liberal legislative agenda. It is calculated and orchestrated by the Mainstream Media to change reality and force down a false narrative.

Rage occurs also when the Narcissist perceives that he is losing or has lost control of his victim. If control is lost, the narcissist will lose his prized scapegoat. If, however, the person no longer enables the fragile, cupcake-like self-image of the Narcissist, the victim must be eliminated. Utter destruction through a Rage Campaign becomes the goal, so the narcissist can move on to a new sacrifice. (If the abused victim has not escaped the failed relationship by this point, it is wise for him to seek refugee status quickly!)

Like a worn-out car or object, the narcissist does not care about this person. The precious pearls of the victim's life, time or attention have already been trampled underfoot. There is no recycling program. Destruction is the only "reasonable" option in the narcissist's mind. Liberal Democrats, in collusion with the Mainstream Media, have also destroyed many lives - literally and physically. Seth Rich, James McDougal, Mary Mahoney, Vince Foster and close to fifty other associates of Bill and Hillary Clinton met early deaths- coincidentally when they were about to testify against the Clintons or had damaging information about them. (Dr. Ronny Jackson merely removed himself from the selection process. At least he is still alive!) Many had suspiciously committed "suicide" by a gunshot wound to the head.

Democrats and Liberals attack their "opponents" with a Rage Campaign, often to destroy them while keeping them alive. This serves as a cautionary lesson for those who dare to oppose the collective mission. "If you do ______, this is what will happen to you- like it did with those other Conservatives." Targets of recent record have been Christian bakers, Aaron and Melissa Klein and former Trump advisor, Michael Caputo.

Oregon bakers, Melissa and Aaron Klein, owned a successful business, Sweetcakes by Melissa. They are also Christian. In 2013, they declined to bake a wedding cake for lesbian couple, Rachel and Laurel Bowman-Cryer on religious grounds: their beliefs did not sanction homosexual marriage. They had previously served homosexuals in their store without incident for many years. This time, for reasons of conscience, they chose not to make the wedding cake for these two women. The lesbian couple filed a complaint with the Oregon Bureau of Labor which led to a media circus, highlighting the details of the case in liberal newscasts.

The Klein family was required to pay thousands of dollars in fines and legal fees. They were eventually forced to close the doors of their business permanently. The rage lawsuit graduated into a Rage Campaign when Social Media provided a platform for the LGBT community to target this couple. Alerted via Facebook and other social platforms, a homo-fascist mob boycotted their business, threatened other wedding vendors in the area and issued death threats to the Klein's children. The lesbian couple received a payment $135,000 from the Klein family in damages.

What happened to the First Amendment rights that guaranteed the free speech and religious liberty of the Klein Family? They could not be controlled by the LGBT agenda, so the Klein family had to be taught a lesson while destroying their business and financial resources.

Another family that was targeted for destruction by left-leaning, Democratic-MSM collusion was that of former Trump advisor, Michael Caputo. On May 2, 2018, Caputo gave testimony to the Mueller Investigation concerning

President Donald Trump and his alleged collusion with Russia during the 2016 election. Caputo testified on behalf of the President in his defense. For this crime, he also entered the crosshairs of Democratic cruelty. He stated that the Investigation forced his family out of their home and crushed his children (they could no longer afford to go to college) because of mounting legal costs associated with the inquiry: "*Today, I can't possibly pay the attendant legal costs and live near my aging father, raising my kids where I grew up,*" Caputo said. *"Your investigation and others into the allegations of Trump campaign collusion with Russia are costing my family a great deal of money — more than $125,000 — and making a visceral impact on my children…Forget about all the death threats against my family. I want to know who cost us so much money, who crushed our kids, who forced us out of our home, all because you lost an election…I want to know because God damn you to hell.*"

https://www.realclearpolitics.com/video/2018/01/16/cory_booker_i_am_frankly_seething_with_anger_over_s-hole_comments_had_tears_of_rage.html

https://www.washingtonexaminer.com/news/god-damn-you-to-hell-michael-caputo-tells-senate-intelligence-in-russia-investigation-testimony

Step 4: Changing Reality

The final step of Narcissistic Gaslighting is to change the reality of the victim. In an individual or with a targeted group, the narcissist purposefully alters facts to cause confusion, question sanity and contradict memory. It is one of the cruelest forms of psychological manipulation possible.

Democratic Liberals have employed similar gaslighting tactics to change the historical narrative via Fake News reported in Mainstream Media outlets. The goal is to cause the American public to question President Donald Trump and evade the detection of their own illegal actions. (FBI Operation Crossfire Hurricane- a book in itself!) By targeting public audiences, they have effectively brought on Trump Derangement Syndrome by their victimizing and exhausting their loyal adherents.

Entire books could be written on President Trump's election win in 2016 and the accusations made in Spygate- when spies were sent to the Trump administration to frame the future president. Throughout investigation, the MSM endlessly accused Russia of interference with the 2016 election by collusion (or help) of Candidate and later President Trump. Both parties insured unfair electoral advantage to President Trump over former candidate, by the leaking of emails of Hillary Clinton. Unfortunately, after two years of Department of Justice investigation, no proof revealed that collusion actually took place. The MSM Russian Collusion narrative, however, continued to be broadcasted anyway as the "true" cause of Clinton's election loss.

The Mueller Investigation, initiated by the FBI, to examine if foreign influence occurred in the US general election, was begun in part due to unsubstantiated media reporting. Volumes as well could be written on the Mueller Investigation and its repercussions in American democracy. The focus of this book, however, is to summarize Fake News items associated with this investigation in terms of gaslighting the American public.

At the one-year anniversary of the Mueller Investigation in May 15, 2018, President Trump tweeted, "*Congratulations America, we are now into the second year of the greatest Witch Hunt in American History ... and there is still No Collusion and No Obstruction. Despite the disgusting, illegal and unwarranted Witch Hunt, we have had the most successful first 17-month Administration in U.S. history -*

by far! The only Collusion was that done by Democrats who were unable to win an Election despite the spending of far more money! Sorry to the Fake News Media and 'Haters,' but that's the way it is!"

The Mueller spokesperson, commenting on the Michael Cohen debacle, warned the press, *"What I have been telling all reporters is that many stories about our investigation have been inaccurate. Be very cautious about any source that claims to have knowledge about our investigation and dig deep into what they claim before reporting on it. If another outlet reports on something, don't run with it unless you have your own sourcing to back this up."*

Why is the Mueller spokesperson giving a class on Journalism 101? Mainstream Media releases on the Mueller Investigation have indeed been numerous. If it is calculated that six, left-leaning TV news outlets- CNN, MSNBC, CBS, ABC, BBC and Reuters reported some aspect on the Mueller Investigation story once every hour, there would have been 52,560 news reports in the first year, conservatively. (Specifically, news stories accusing President Trump of some aspect of Russian Collusion.)

At the one-year mark of the Mueller Investigation, at the revelation of the Trump targeting, covert FBI operation, Crossfire Hurricane, it was determined that the Russian Collusion narrative had been false the entire time. That was enough fake news to last a lifetime!

Mainstream Media newscasters, desperately proclaiming a false narrative, led the American public down a fictitious rabbit hole, openly promoting distrust and hatred for the duly elected President. They altered facts to cause confusion. False reports were reinforced over and over so that viewers believed an "altered reality." Nationwide gaslighting, initiated by Democratic leadership and orchestrated by the Mainstream Media occurred to subjugate Americans under a Deep-State and tyrannical power base.

---

http://www.foxnews.com/opinion/2017/12/28/oregon-court-rules-christian-bakery-must-pay-135g-to-lesbian-couple.

https://www.washingtonexaminer.com/news/god-damn-you-to-hell-michael-caputo-tells-senate-intelligence-in-russia-investigation-testimony

https://www.washingtontimes.com/news/2018/apr/16/rober
t-mueller-many-news-stories-trump-russia-prob/
https://www.newsbusters.org/blogs/nb/rich-noyes/2018/05/
08/media-get-trumped-presidents-polls-improve-despite-9
0-negative

http://dailycaller.com/2018/04/16/michael-cohen-prague-m
eeting/

Chapter 9
The Religion of Narcissism

Trump Derangement Syndrome is usually not associated with religious groups. This is most likely because President Trump is not overtly religious. Democrats, however, routinely target religious organizations and people. Many times, however, religious populations are proportionately more conservative leaning: Pro-Life organizations especially.

If a Christian does not make a wedding cake for a homosexual couple or if a religious organization supports an oppositional view to Democratic agenda, they run the risk of being punished by a rageful mob. Mob tactics here are similar to those seen at Trump Derangement Syndrome-like demonstrations. Why? What is it about these groups that bring about such a response?

Democrats claim to be tolerant. The Democratic Platform of 2016 reads, *"We will do everything we can to protect religious minorities and the fundamental right of freedom of religion."* However, in practice, not every religious group receives the same treatment- namely Christians and Jews.

Christian groups have often been targeted by the Obama Administration by its weaponization of the IRS to audit their books. Lawsuits and heavy fines were imposed on individuals and groups who refused to give up their free expression of beliefs. If the Democratic Party heralds the freedom of religious tolerance, why would they target religious groups?

The average narcissist aims to be everything that God is: omniscient (all knowing), omnipotent (all powerful), omnipresent (everywhere present) and in general, the center of the known universe. The Granddaddy of all narcissists, however, was a perfectly created angel who once went by the name of Lucifer. In the Bible, Lucifer was the highest ranking and the most beautiful of all God's created angels. Ezekiel 28:11-15 describes him best:

"Thus saith the Lord GOD; Thou sealest up the sum, full of wisdom, and perfect in beauty. Thou hast been in Eden the garden of God; every precious stone was thy covering, the sardius, topaz, and the diamond, the beryl, the onyx, and the jasper, the sapphire, the emerald, and the carbuncle, and gold: the workmanship of thy tabrets and of thy pipes was prepared in thee in the day that thou wast created. Thou art the anointed cherub that covereth; and I have set thee so: thou wast upon the holy mountain of God; thou hast walked up and down in the midst of the stones of fire."

This angel was something else! He was perfect in beauty and knew it. He was covered with precious stones. As the Angel of Light, he must have been quite the display of color when light shone through him. He also walked among the "stones of fire." Some Biblical scholars believe that this meant Lucifer had access to pre-earth planning meetings or predeterminate counsels. He attended meetings on the Holy Mountain and later communicated news items to the rest of the heavenly host. (It was the CNN-Celestial News Network) In addition, Lucifer sang of God's praises with his "pipes and tabrets."

It all went south-literally. Beginning in verse 15, because of the free choice of Lucifer: *"Thou wast perfect in thy ways from the day that thou wast created, till iniquity was found in thee… Thine heart was lifted up because of thy beauty, thou hast corrupted thy wisdom by reason of thy brightness: I will cast thee to the ground, I will lay thee before kings, that they may behold thee."* Lucifer became stuck on himself; his heart became proud because of his beauty. He decided that he needed to replace God because he was more magnificent and better qualified. It didn't stop there. Lucifer acted out on his self-love in Isaiah 14: *"How you have fallen from heaven, morning star, son of the dawn! …You said in your heart, "I will ascend to the heavens; I will raise my throne above the stars of God; I will ascend above the tops of the clouds; I will make myself like the Most High."*

The result of Lucifer's approbation was described by Jesus Christ in Luke 10:18: *"I saw Satan fall like lightning from Heaven."* Does this sound familiar? The key take-away from these verses is that Lucifer, the Granddaddy of all Narcissists, wanted God, his Maker, go on a permanent vacation. God's services, in Lucifer's opinion, were no longer required on the Holy Mountain. This awesome angel was running the universe now! The problem was that God was not taking applications for new members of the Trinity.

Kudos to Dan Bongino's podcast that first inspired this chain of thought: Democratic Leadership also seeks to offer up their ruling services to the world. They want to provide universal healthcare. They want to bring about a world of truth, justice and social equality. They want to save the environment. They want to take these values and teach them to future generations. There is nothing wrong with these goals. The problem is that they want to replace God in people's lives. They want to replace the administration of services: they want to swap out who is doing the saving. They try to offer anything people could ever need or want. They become vengeful towards those who don't play along.

How do Democratic Liberals accomplish this swap? What are they swapping specifically? They exchange individual rights for the common good of all. The Founding Fathers wrote the Constitution to form "a more perfect Union." Early in the document, however, the freedom and rights of INDIVIDUALS were outlined and declared in the Bill of Rights. The Bill of Rights safeguard individual freedoms of American citizens, *"in order to prevent misconstruction or abuse of its powers."* The wise Framers of the Constitution realized that when individual freedoms were compromised, the common good of the nation would be undermined.

Democrat leadership wants freedom, but under a new set of terms. They seek, because of socialist perspective, the COLLECTIVE good. This is the exact opposite of what the Framers of the Constitution had in mind. Democrats want Americans to be dependent on government (or them while in office) to provide welfare, government programs, healthcare, education and regulations. To them, individual freedoms are only useful if they are yielded to the common good. It is a substitute system, like the old model, only "evolved." It is similar, but fundamentally different.

Christianity and Judaism are different from other religions because they place emphasis on an individual's relationship with God. Romans 14:4 states: *to his own master he standeth or falleth. Yea, he shall be holden up: for God is able to make him stand.* The laws of Moses were written for the nation of Israel, but individuals were expected to carry them out. The Protestant Reformation was all about rejecting the power and control of the collective (at that time), Roman Catholic Church system in favor of individual faith: *"for it is written, the just will live by faith."*

Romans 1:17. The word "just" here is the Greek word, *dikaios*, meaning a **singular**, just man. This word is used in Matthew 1:19, for example, to describe Joseph, the step father of Jesus: *"Then Joseph her husband, being a just MAN, and not willing to make her a public example, was minded to put her (Mary, when found to be pregnant and unmarried) away privily."*

Judaism is one of the world's first monotheistic religions. When ancient Samaria, Assyria, Egypt, Greece and Rome were worshiping many gods, the Jews worshiped one; His name was Yahweh. The Shema, the centerpiece of Jewish prayer, reads, *"Hear O Israel, the Lord is Our God, the Lord is One."* The first law of the Ten Commandments of Moses is, *"I am the Lord your God. You shall have no other gods before me,"* in Exodus 20:2. Set apart by God through the seed of Abraham, the Jewish nation was the chosen instrument of God to be the *"light unto the Gentiles, that my salvation may reach to the ends of the earth,"* in Isaiah 49:6. Jewish people have paid dearly for this mission via persecution for roughly each generation of its existence. Throughout history, the Jews have resolutely refused to worship anything in the creation of God in the place of their Creator.

The Mainstream Media has had plenty of practice attacking such rebellious religious groups. One such infamous and historical Rage Campaign began in 1933, in Berlin, Germany, when an insignificant corporal named Adolph Hitler was elected to be the Chancellor of Germany. Hitler blamed the Jews for Germany's loss of World War I, even though many of them had died fighting for that land. He also believed that some races (his) were superior, and others were inferior. The Jews, Hitler believed, were one of the most offensive, inferior races, a parasite that fed on the neck of mankind. They also refused to bow down to Hitler. The only solution to this problematic people was to round them up and kill them.

How did he accomplish the genocide of the Jewish People? The Nazi had a press corps, the Wehrmacht, which helped Hitler accomplish this evil agenda. By 1945, Hitler had rounded up 6 million European Jews for slaughter during the Holocaust. He used two tools to accomplish this: his secret police force, the Gestapo, and his news propaganda machine.

A narcissist himself, Hitler adjusted facts, to gaslight Germany into accepting his agenda. He stated in his autobiography, Mein Kampf, *"If you tell a big enough lie and tell it frequently enough, it will be believed. Make the*

lie big, make it simple, and eventually they will believe it."
Nazis simply told lies about the Jewish people.
Newspapers and films routinely circulated Hitler's
anti-Semitic propaganda around the Third Reich. It was
one of the worst blights on journalistic history that has ever
been recorded.

How did the Nazi propaganda machine do it? Headed by
Josef Goebbels, the press corps was first developed to
advertise and embellish the Nazi war effort. By 1942, there
were 15,000 members of this military propaganda
organization. The Jews were commonly reported on along
with the war effort. They were more often reported on,
however, during times of battlefront lulls. (Creating news
when there is no news.)

<u>Der Sturmer</u>, a weekly Nazi tabloid, maligned the Jews
with anti-Semitic quotes such as this: *"As elsewhere, the
Jews here [in Minsk] constitute a real danger. They are
our enemies at all times. And want to be. It's still possible
to find former commissars in the ghetto. This is the origin
of their constant desire to disturb the population. But using
all means possible, we will crush the resistance of the
Jews. It is common knowledge that before their
withdrawal, the Soviets spared the ghetto when setting fire
to the town. A clear solution to the Jewish Question in this*

region is the precondition for future peace and calm here… enemies of mankind, who are able only to destroy, not to create. Communism is an Asian phenomenon influenced by the Jews, and aspires to plunge culture and civilization, created with such huge effort, back into the depths of the most primitive form of human existence.

Nazi reporters energetically churned out propaganda directed against Jewish people who lived in the ghettos. Jewish Historian, Daniel Uziel wrote, *"After the invasion of Poland, the Propaganda Ministry was asked by the German press to provide photos of Jews; it passed on the request to the military's Propaganda Department. On October 2, 1939, the PKs stationed in Poland received the following order from the Propaganda Ministry in Berlin: Of high priority is film footage showing all sorts of Jewish types. We need more than before, from Warsaw and all the occupied territories. What we want are portraits and images of Jews at work. This material is to be used to reinforce our anti-Semitic propaganda at home and abroad."* Once information was accumulated, Jewish ghetto occupants were later described in the pamphlet, <u>The Jew as World Parasite</u>: *"The German people has recognized that the Jew has crept in like a parasite not only into our people, but into all the peoples of the earth, and that it is attempting to corrupt the original racial characteristics of the peoples in order to destroy them both racially and as states, and thereby rule over them…The Jew is the parasite of humanity. He can be a parasite for an individual person, a social parasite for whole peoples, and the world parasite of humanity."*

 Ludwig Fischer, the governor of Warsaw reported that "3,000 large posters, 7,000 smaller posters, and 500,000 pamphlets" were distributed to inform Polish citizens of the health risks presented by living too close to the ghetto. It was easy afterwards to justify their extinction. They were rebels who refused to swallow Nazi guidelines to replace God with a man.

Hitler was not alone to promote Rage Campaigns via the press; Josef Stalin, Mao Tse Tung, Kim Jong-il, Saddam Hussein and many other narcissistic dictators used propaganda to keep themselves in power. The newspapers, *Pravda* (in the Soviet Union) and *The Red Flag* (in Communist China), for example, were unashamedly tools used by leaders to re-educate or intimidate the working classes towards the goals of the autonomous collective.

Personal relationship and responsibility, on the other hand, is emphasized in Judeo- Christian beliefs. Other religions do not share this. (Abraham, for example, was the *friend of God*" in Genesis 18. Jesus encouraged his disciples to call God the Father, "Abba" or Daddy.) Buddhist and Hindu Nirvana adherents meld at death into a universal bliss of nothingness. The Islamic faith operates by rules but not by a personal relationship of a loving, Father-God. This concept is unknown in Islamic faith.

The relational aspect of Judeo-Christian beliefs is, therefore, unique. Both faiths are commanded to obey **God first**. Obedience to one's fellow man comes in **second place.** Democrats and Liberals do not like this; like all narcissists, they want control. They seek to bring down anything that would dare come between them and the masses.

President Obama led the charge to control disobedient Christian groups when he weaponized the Internal Revenue Service to target fundamentalist groups. In 2013, the IRS admitted that it had selected "Tea Party" and "conservative" groups for investigation because of their names. The inquiries centered around the tax-exempt status of the organizations. Because churches were under tax-exempt status, they also came under investigation. This issue developed into a full-on, Obama scandal.

Citizens faced the possible revocation of their tax-exempt status, were accused of tax evasion or fraud, and were forced to pay heavy fines. They also could be required to their reveal donor lists which had been- up to that point-redacted from public view. The Billy Graham Evangelistic Association and the humanitarian organization, Samaritan's Purse, under Franklin Graham, was subjected to review by the IRS during this controversy. In 2013, the IRS notified these two organizations that it was conducting a "review" of tax activities for the year 2010. Graham said that he believed that the IRS was "targeting and attempting to intimidate us."

Why? The Billy Graham Evangelical Association encouraged voters to back *"candidates who base their decisions on biblical principles and support the nation of Israel."* IRS agents visited the organization's headquarters in North Carolina after the re-election of President Obama, Graham affirmed. Mr. Graham wrote to President Obama on this matter saying: *"Mr. President, the IRS has already publicly acknowledged it operated in a less than neutral and non-partisan way. We also now know that the target of their improper actions was much wider than political or Tea Party organizations. Will you take some immediate action to reassure Americans we are not in a new chapter of American history – repressive government rule?"*

Christians who failed to comply with Obamacare mandates also found themselves targeted by the Democratic Leadership. Another religious group targeted by Obama's health care agenda was The Little Sisters of the Poor. The Little Sisters of the Poor, an order of Catholic nuns, operate a charitable organization that serves the elderly-poor in thirty countries around the world. Irrespective of race or religion, the sisters provide homes for this needy population. It also receives federal funds to carry out these services.

When Obamacare was enacted, however, the Sisters were forced to provide contraception and abortion-inducing drugs to their employees under their health insurance coverage. The Little Sisters refused to comply because doing so would "violate their faith" in distributing contraception. They, like many formidable nuns throughout history (including mine), challenged this requirement by lawsuit. The Supreme Court ruled in their behalf on May 16, 2016. They were small, but mighty! The Sisters won exemption from the mandate and the costs of their lawsuit process were reimbursed.

The fact that these nuns were indicted **at all** is significant. Who requires celibate nuns that work with elderly (and clearly past contraception needs) to give out birth control? The Little Sisters of the Poor and the Billy Graham Evangelical Association, however, share a secret. They do not look for leadership from outside of their organizations. They answer to a Higher Power. They encourage others to do the same and are not afraid to push back if their rights are threatened. This is an affront to Democrats who crave citizens to flock under their wings of protection like little chicks.

The Mainstream Media also campaigns against religiously affiliated business. Another faith-based group under recent media attack has been the restaurant chain, Chick Fil-A. It's founder, Truett Cathy, long ago (1946) made the decision to close his chicken sandwich shops on Sunday because he saw, *"the importance of closing on Sundays so that he and his employees could set aside one day to rest and worship if they choose."*

Cathy's son, Dan Cathy in 2012 made a public statement in support of traditional marriage saying: *"I think the time of truths and principles are captured and codified in God's word and I'm just personally committed to that...We are very much supportive of the family — the biblical definition of the family unit. We are a family-owned business, a family-led business, and we are married to our first wives. We give God thanks for that...we know that it might not be popular with everyone, but thank the Lord, we live in a country where we can share our values and operate on biblical principles...I know others feel very different from that and I respect their opinion and I hope that they would be respectful of mine."*

Cathy's belief was, according to the Mainstream Media viewpoint, a stance against equal rights of the LGBTQ/same sex community. Chick Fil-A became a media target because of these two standpoints. <u>Forbes</u> magazine had already labeled Chick Fil-A a "cult" in 2006 for closing on Sunday.

After Cathy made his traditional marriage statements, the gloves really came off. According to the Huffington Post, Chick Fil-A was "anti-gay" and "questionable." *"How backward and ignorant ... how sad,"* CNN reader Joe Brown said. *"No more Chick-fil-A for me. I am not in the stone-casting business..."* Social media started a wave of protest when it rallied the LGBTQ community to hold kiss-ins at Chick Fil-A stores. The New York Times wrote a story in April 2018, describing the opening of a Chick-fil A store as "*a creepy infiltration*" as though the makers of chicken sandwiches had emerged from a zombie apocalypse or alien spaceship.

Lucifer, the fallen angel, sought to replace God. He would destroy God's people or anything else that would keep him from the throne of power. Narcissists mirror this behavior. Many Democratic leaders want Big Government control. It is not surprising when they become hostile towards groups promoting, in their minds, "harmful" beliefs. Christians and Jewish groups seem to detect Big Government control and say, "No thanks. Pass." The resulting display of narcissistic anger rivals any rage seen on a college campus or derangement expressed against the President himself. The narcissist would do well to remember that with Lucifer, the attempt to seize power did not end well.

https://www.yadvashem.org/articles/academic/wehrmacht-propaganda-troops-and-the-jews.html

https://www.ushmm.org/wlc/en/article.php?ModuleId=10007819

http://research.calvin.edu/german-propaganda-archive/weltparasit.htm

https://www.huffingtonpost.com/2012/07/17/dan-cathy-chick-fil-a-president-anti-gay_n_1680984.html

https://www.cnn.com/2012/07/27/us/chick-fil-a-controversy/index.html

Chapter 10
Conservatism is Good for You!

If narcissists are continually on the lookout for new victims to bolster their fragile self-egos, how can one protect themselves from their cloak-and-dagger methodology? How can a person avoid the pitfalls of stumbling into a narcissistic relationship? Remember, a narcissist can be a lot of fun to be around. They ooze charm. They cause their victims to believe that they are worth the grief that they inflict.

Being a conservative in many ways can help a person not to become ensnared by a Narcissist. Conservative principles can help protect you. Conservatism is good for you! This is because Conservative values highly the rights of an individual. Conservatives, as people, appreciate the cost of freedom that was paid by brave men that put on their boots and marched onto a battlefield. They work hard for their bread and enjoy the fruits of their labor. They are proud of their country much in the same way as they are proud of their mother; Mom might have her faults, but to the conservative, she's a Rockstar. Because they love Mom and their country, they will not hesitate to defend her if necessary.

Democratic Liberals value the rights of individuals with conditions. Again, the individual is demanded to sacrifice individual freedoms for the good of the collective group or the people who lead that group. People are allowed the freedom of their beliefs **but are tightly controlled in expressing them** if they disagree with party policy.

Democrats apologize for the pain America has caused throughout history and in recent memory. (Nobody's perfect, right?) Workers must fork over the fruit of their labor to this leadership control via tax increases. They too love the USA, but Freudian-style, blame their political parents, Lady Liberty and Uncle Sam, for their individual failures and internal problems. The Founding Fathers are likewise targeted, very much like an angry teenager who has been denied the car keys.

Because any narcissist is enticing, preventative safeguards are necessary to their unsuspecting and innocent targets. Conservative principles can act as a protective armor against ensnaring their tactics and abuse. Here are 7 Conservative principles to help keep oneself from the snare of the narcissist:

1. Have a Good Self-Image

Are you free or the victim of tyranny? The Democratic Liberal is normally the victim of someone else. They are victims of slavery, class warfare, a failed educational system, society, the failed criminal justice system, capitalists, corporation carbon footprints-the list expands with each generation.

Conservatives, on the other hand are free. They are busy with life, liberty and the pursuit of happiness. Any child born can be President or be anything he wants to be in the land of opportunity. In America, citizens are free to pursue the American dream and work hard to attain it. Conservatives enjoy the challenge to overcome the odds stacked against them. Freedom starts in the mind. They can walk away or fight if personal freedom is threatened. Narcissists have a harder time sucking free thinkers into quicksand.

2. Conservatives Know Their Rights

To avoid a narcissist, a person must have a firm sense of personal rights and boundaries. When a narcissist (or any other scoundrel) crosses the line to limit personal freedom, individual rights must be indelibly imprinted on a person's mind to withstand the onslaught. Conservatives excel at knowing their rights. They love the Bill of Rights! They value their personal property and will defend it.

It is a different story with Democrats or Liberals. They can personally own a car so long as it's a Prius and not harmful to the environment. They can own a home if it has solar panels. They embrace victimhood, carrying signs and highlighting causes on the nightly news. They demand their rights in defense of a group: big business, unsustainable greenhouse offenders, or the racially downtrodden. Defense of such groups give them direction and money. Chasing the causes also help to relieve the "stress" of Trump Derangement Syndrome.

If a conservative knows their rights, however, they will be less likely to give them up to an alluring narcissist.

3. Conservatives Protect Their Rights

Because they know their rights, conservatives are more likely to protect their rights. Most conservatives keenly aware of their Second Amendment rights to bear arms. When the narcissist attempts to cross the line of personal freedoms, the Conservative has options. They fight back and protect their intellectual or personal property.

4. Conservatives Question Tyranny

In the spirit of our Forebears, who questioned the right of King George III and the British Empire to govern and tax the American colonies without representation, Conservatives are also great at questioning tyranny. Each Fourth of July, America celebrates the throwing off of tyrants and declaring personal freedoms. Thomas Jefferson penned The Declaration of Independence with this core belief in mind.

Conservatives respect authority, but have no problem questioning it when the line of personal freedom is crossed. Narcissists, on the other hand, do not want their authority questioned under any circumstances. Being a conservative will afford a potential victim with a mindset that questions and therefore limits coercion of unrestrained authority.

5. Conservatives Resist Grooming

The Narcissist likes to groom his or her victim with excessive praise and approval. He tells this person that he is truly the "best person on the planet" because he wants something. Lulled by soothing waves of flattery, the internal guard is let down. Conservatives, on the other hand, tend to know who they are and don't need to be groomed.

President Trump is a good example of a person who is not in need of grooming. He knew who he was before he ran for office: a successful businessman and TV celebrity. He did not need politicians to help him up the DC ladder. He simply took advantage of the opportunities available to every American.

6. Conservatives Maintain Balanced Relationships

Conservatives love the Declaration of Independence which states, "All men are created equal." They embrace and celebrate the fact that the ground of freedom every American citizen stands upon is even. For the Conservative, individual rights are equally irrevocable. Conservatives, therefore, tend to gravitate towards more balanced relationships, based on mutual respect.

Democratic Liberals, on the other hand, seem to favor a savior-victim, codependency. This model displays a leader who is constantly rescuing someone or something who is oppressed. The narcissist, because he is such an exceptional person, plays the role of savior; the other person in the relationship becomes the transgressed victim- whether he has asked for salvation or not. The sell job begins.

7. Conservatives Are Less Likely to Manipulate

Because they value personal freedom and individual rights, Conservatives are less likely manipulate. They allow other citizens the right to enjoy the same liberty that they enjoy. Conservatives dislike being imposed upon.

Democrats and Liberals, however, have no problem imposing their agendas on others, particularly if they think their cause is a good one. Again, because they tend to sacrifice individual freedom on the altar of the collective good, they value submission. In the hands of a narcissist, this type of behavior can degenerate quickly. Submission turns into slavery; justifications can deteriorate into gaslighting.

For the above stated reasons, being a Conservative is good for you!

Chapter 11
How to Lose a Narcissist

One great tip to rid oneself of a Narcissist, beyond holding firm to conservative principles, is simple: ask the Narcissist many, many questions. When the narcissist reveals his or her interests, choose one and ask hundreds of questions about it.

For example, if the Narcissist likes to fish, ask "What kind of fish do you catch? Where do you buy your worms? What do you use for bait? What time of the day do you fish? What kind of rod do you use? Do you have a lure collection? Do you fish from a boat or from the shore?"

Salt and pepper this person with questions. If the narcissist is lying about his or her talents, there will be a contradiction in the answers somewhere. This is a red flag. Why is this person lying?

Even if the Narcissist is not lying, he or she will still run away from you because narcissists cannot stand to be questioned or scrutinized. He will quickly move off in search of a more naïve victim.

The same questioning technique can throw off a Liberal Democrat or activist. They cannot endure specific and numerous questions. Anti-gun activists, for example, regularly avoid those who question their beliefs.

Actress, Alyssa Milano (Kudos again to Dan Bongino's NRATV broadcast, We Stand, for highlighting this story), for example, staged a small protest near the NRA Convention in Dallas, Texas in May of 2018. NRA members, walking through the protest area with children, confronted Milano asking questions: *"Are your security guards armed? Would you (to Alyssa) come on NRA TV and bridge the divide here? We would love to talk to you Alyssa, we would! Do you feel that way about Planned Parenthood? So, your organization is a group of like-minded people coming together to influence people?*

That's what we do, the NRA. You know, I am not confrontational?" After wishing the NRA members well, Ms. Milano quickly fled the anti-gun protest with her heavily armed entourage. To smoke a Liberal, Democrat or activist, pepper-spray them with questions and watch them run!

It is a terrible thing to accuse someone-anybody of being narcissist. Because my family and I have personally suffered from the effects of a narcissist, I would not judge Alyssa Milano to be one. I do not know her personally. Ms. Milano's right to freely protest is guaranteed in the First Amendment to the Constitution.

Why do activists, however, run from being seriously questioned or when presented with opposing facts? Milano accused the NRA members of being "incredibly confrontational" when, in fact they were being insistent, but polite. Milano was not being threatened, but she was being questioned. If the activist or Democratic leader is in earnest, why can't he or she do their homework and answer questions in a rigorous debate? Some do, but most retreat into safe spaces. Perhaps they do not want to look bad because they are unprepared. They do, however, want the world to see them during a protest demonstration.

Human beings are designed for intimacy. We are not designed to be alone. We must be careful about how we satisfy these needs, however. My mother, for example, wanted to find a great husband in a time when few were available. She was afraid she would be an old maid with no children. When my Dad with narcissist personality disorder showed up, he sold himself to her as top-of-the-line goods. He utilized compliments to win the prize. He did not, however, show respect for her interests, privacy or friends. Mom did not ask enough questions. My suspicion is that she did not want to know the downside of her "prince." Choosing to ignore these red flags, she let herself ride the wave of love that came along with devastating consequences.

Devastating consequences follow narcissists wherever they go. If they are found in the governments, an entire nations can be hijacked. By holding fast to the principles of liberty and freedom for all, those same nations can be preserved. Conservative principles that honor mutual respect of individuals can translate over into protection of personal freedoms in relationships. The dynamics are identical. Healthy relationships are not afraid of dialogue and to answer questions. We can seek to find an intimate relationship without extinguishing who we are.

https://www.youtube.com/watch?v=aoYs_3kSc0g

Conclusion

Narcissism Personality Disorder is a dangerous psychological condition. It is also tragic because the person that suffers from this disorder has been severely criticized or abused to the point where he or she cannot tolerate criticism. (Thank you, Dr. Spock!) They have been reduced to feeding on affirmation and shun-mostly from a perceived threat of self-preservation- any sort of evaluation. Narcissism is a severe disorder that requires equally severe intervention.

The Narcissistic Spectrum Narcissists are very diverse. They can be identified on a spectrum. The Narcissistic Spectrum begins with the least offensive narcissist- the

quiet, Closet Narcissist and is followed by the Know-It-All
(wise guy) Narcissist, who a self-proclaimed expert on
everything. Following the Wise Guy Narcissist is the
Casanova Narcissist, whose job is to groom and entice
unsuspecting victims into their self-absorbed lair. Next
comes the Tyrant Narcissist who bullies others nearby or
online. Lastly is the Toxic Narcissist who employs the
most abusive of all psychological manipulation:
gaslighting.

While all these narcissists cause harm, the Toxic
Narcissist is the most dangerous of them all and is to be
avoided in unbroken run. See diagram below:

Narcissistic Spectrum

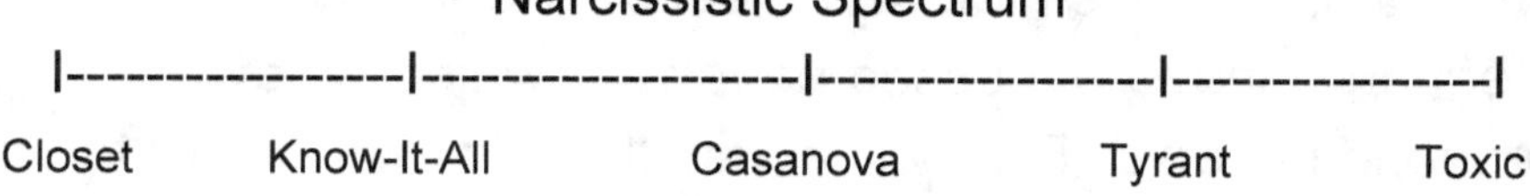

Many people have narcissistic, self-loving tendencies and
fall somewhere on the above diagram based on their
outward behaviors. The Selfie Generation was not made
overnight. There have been decades of Progressivist
activists infiltrating American classrooms, airwaves and
child-rearing manuals. The great generation of World War
II, where Americans, survived the Great Depression,
sacrificed for the American war effort and knew how to "go
without" is slowly dying out. The election of Donald Trump

is seen by some as a "last ditch effort" to bring back these vital skills and values. I hope it works.

For now, Conservatives must share their living space with Democrats, Liberals and activists- enduring their repeated onslaughts and advances. President Trump did not cause their angst; he merely revealed a culture that had already been growing when he didn't need the praise of men to be successful. Trump Derangement Syndrome is merely a symptom of a greater need and a greater problem: narcissism and narcissistic tendencies.

Some claim that the mythological Narcissus drowned while trying to kiss his own reflection. As a former lifeguard, I have witnessed people drowning. They respond in panic. They will do anything in their power to climb on top of the rescuer to stay afloat and near oxygen. The lifeguard must wait for the thrashing and struggling to lessen or there will be two drowning victims: the swimmer and the lifeguard.

Trump Derangement Syndrome, in my opinion, mimics this sort of panic response. Democratic Liberals truly believe their policies and/or lives are in danger. As lifeguard conservatives, we must wait them out. We need to wait until they are ready to be rescued after they panic.

Every Socialist regime has fallen; failure of Liberal agenda is imminent. Margaret Thatcher once said: *"The problem with socialism is that you eventually run out of other people's money."*

As we wait for our Democratic and Liberal fellow citizens to exhaust themselves, drowning themselves in ideology that they helplessly cling to, we must ask them many thought-provoking questions. We must sometimes walk away when necessary. Other times, we stand up against their demands. In the spirit of the Founding Fathers, we must hold all men to the established system of checks and balances that were designed to protect all of our freedoms. Only then can we prevent them and ourselves from drowning into the pool of Democratic, Selfie-Generation Narcissism. They need us.